MAGICAL HISTORY TOUR

The 1960s Revisited

MAGICAL HISTORY TOUR

The 1960s Revisited

STUART HYLTON

Sutton Publishing

First published in the United Kingdom in 2000 by
Sutton Publishing Limited · Phoenix Mill
Thrupp · Stroud · Gloucestershire · GL5 2BU

British Library Cataloguing in Publication Data
A catalogue record for this book is available from the British Library.

ISBN 0-7509-2253-2

Typeset in 10/13 pt Sabon.
Typesetting and origination by
Sutton Publishing Limited.
Printed and bound in England by
J.H. Haynes & Co. Ltd, Sparkford.

CONTENTS

PREFACE AND ACKNOWLEDGEMENTS

One of my wilder ideas for the title of this book was a line from Philip Larkin's poem *Annus Mirabilis*: 'Sexual intercourse began in 1963'. Every generation believes that theirs is the first to discover the joys of the flesh and this was never more true than in the case of the children of the 1960s. However, the publishers were mindful of the misunderstandings that could flow from this. For one thing, the book could have ended up on the bookseller's top shelf, alongside *The Art of Sensual Massage* and Delia Smith's *101 More Things to do with Chocolate*. Imagine the disappointment of connoisseurs of sexual intercourse everywhere, carrying the book home in its plain wrapper, only to open it at the pages dealing with Sir Alec Douglas-Home. (This may well be the first time in the history of the English language that the words *sexual intercourse* and *Sir Alec Douglas-Home* have appeared in the same sentence.)

Instead, it became *Magical History Tour*. If you carelessly misread the title as 'Magical Mystery Tour', and bought this book under the impression that you were getting some kind of exposé of the Beatles' drug-culture years, full of sex and scandal, you may be luckier than you had any right to expect. I may not know much about history, but I know what I like. When I drew up a list of possible contents for the book, I realised that I was potentially talking about a whole shelf-full of publications, for this was the decade when the old world and the new collided. The rock and roll generation discarded many of its parents' traditional values, in art, dress and (to use a hideous term that was itself probably a 1960s invention) lifestyle. New technology began to take over – as the final steam trains were puffing to extinction and the last great passenger liner was launched, we saw the beginnings of supersonic passenger flight and the first men setting foot on the moon. Computers ceased to be the toys of scientists and started messing up our lives in a serious way. There were scandals enough to keep several decades frothing with moral indignation, though people were increasingly disinclined to be outraged by them. Race relations reached new heights of tension and many in Britain began to reassess our nation's role in the world. The decade seemed to be populated by more than its share of larger-than-life characters – from the Kray twins, Peter Rachman and Emil Savundra at one end of the moral spectrum, to Mary Whitehouse, John F. Kennedy and the Bishop of Woolwich at the other. (Mary Whitehouse would probably tell me that I've put the Bishop of Woolwich at the wrong end of the spectrum. Others have their suspicions about Mary Whitehouse).

From this wealth of material I selected the people and incidents that I remembered or that rang bells in the minds of those I talked to about the project. I tried to steer clear of some of the most frequently recounted events, so the book cannot claim to cover all the most important landmarks of the decade. Or, to put it another way, my selection is perfectly wilful, arbitrary and unrepresentative – just like the decade itself.

Particular thanks for permission to use illustrations go to the following copyright holders, including some fellow Sutton authors: Ray Bailey (pp. 128, 129), British Aerospace (p. 137), Buckinghamshire Records and Local Studies Service (pp. 95, 128, 129), Cunard (pp. 143, 144, 145), David Cuppleditch (from *Lincoln – the Twentieth Century*) (p. 54), Anthony Kersting (p. 95), London Borough of Hammersmith and Fulham (p. 157), London Borough of Hammersmith and Fulham/Mrs C. Bayliss (p. 157), Chris Grabham and the Luton Museum Service (pp. 4, 7, 8, 47, 53, 54, 60, 61, 69, 75, 76, 82, 83, 86, 88, 102, 103, 108, 115, 121, 135, 148), City of Nottingham (Local Studies Library collection) (p. 20), Reading Museum (Reading Borough Council) (pp. 44, 49), Richard Reed (pp. 6, 7, 8, 9, 10, 11, 14, 27, 38, 43, 48, 53, 54, 60, 64, 73, 84, 92, 93, 95, 101, 110, 114, 117, 120, 121, 122, 130, 151, 161, 170) and West Sussex County Council Record Office (pp. 2, 3, 31, 91). If I have forgotten anybody in the long and arduous business of gathering the illustrations, my apologies and thanks go to you as well.

CHAPTER 1

BE THERE OR BE SQUARE: 1960s FASHION AND LIFESTYLE

We must accept that young people express themselves in new manners of dress that may seem queer to the older of us.
The Archbishop of Canterbury, contemplating topless dresses

The 1960s was the decade in which the cult of youth came – if this is not a contradiction in terms – to full maturity. Young people had money and the leisure to spend it. The security of full employment and relative peace during the 1950s gave them the confidence to assert themselves and their ideas. Hedonism became more than enjoyable – it was presented as socially useful, liberating and important. A cartoon of the day showed a pop star demanding sexual favours from his girlfriend with the words: 'I wish to follow the dictates of my conscience.' The standard joke about the drug-fuelled indulgences of the decade was that if you could remember the 'swinging sixties' then you weren't there. But for many people at the time it seemed that it was always someone else – someone older, younger, more streetwise, more sophisticated, better off or less hung up on material things – who was having the really good time that was portrayed in the media.

Egalitarian ideals were preached, but there was a new form of social pecking order, based on fashion and lifestyle. A new aristocracy – of disc jockeys, photographers, pop stars and fashion designers – came into being, and it was quite an exclusive caste. John Peel recalls once questioning why a record by Country Joe and the Fish was not in the charts, since everyone he knew had a copy. It was only later he realised he'd got it the wrong way round – he knew everyone who had a copy. The most unexpected people felt that they were not part of the in-crowd. Julie Christie – star, among other things, of the cult 1960s film *Darling* – talked about feeling like a country bumpkin among the glamorous society in which she found herself

Julie Christie, 1960s film icon, on the set of the film Darling.

moving, not knowing how to deal with her fame. In the remainder of this chapter, we look at some of the fashion statements of the day and at the reactions of wider society to the new forms of self-expression adopted by the young. But first we consider the changing moral climate that gave rise to the image of 'Swinging London'.

SWINGING LONDON

It is possible to date the term 'Swinging London' to an article in the *New York Times* in May 1966. This suggested that Britain (rather narrowly defined as the area between Soho and the Kings Road) had become the new Sodom and Gomorrah. London, its readers were told, was now the kind of place where a senior official could dance the watusi without the Baptist Church demanding his (or her) resignation (a fate that had recently befallen American presidential advisor Bill Moyers for some ill-advised fancy footwork at the Smithsonian Museum in Washington). The evangelist Billy Graham was said to be packing to come and save London from its excesses. Moreover, British fashion gurus visiting New York were told that American men were far too conservative to go for the Beau

A possible early outbreak of the hippie tendency? Bill Napier and his Hawaiians, Worthing, 1960.

Brummell fashions that they were trying to promote – this from the land that was about to give us the hippie. The pendulum had swung – no longer seen as reserved, stiff and prudish, we now had a reputation for permissiveness. This suggestion cut British sensibilities to the quick. Used for decades to being regarded as the boring men of Europe, to be suddenly thought of as interesting was more than some could bear. The government was worried that the perception of us as a nation of party animals could have horrific effects on the international currency market, bringing overnight parity with the lira. The strangest of bedfellows were recruited to reassure the world that Britain was still reliably dull and sensible, including the London correspondent of the Russian newspaper *Izvestia*.

DEDICATED FOLLOWERS OF FASHION

The 1960s will be remembered for the variety – and in many cases the extremity – of its fashions, as young people began to differentiate themselves dramatically from the oldies. The early 1960s saw the introduction of the mini-skirt, which was popularised, if not actually introduced, by Mary Quant. The other person who bore a share of the

morley BRI NYLON **TIGHTS**

FREEDOM
FOR
GIRLS

TIGHTS FOR LADIES AND CHILDREN
IN VARIOUS COLOURS

Mossop & Hunt Ltd.
16 GROVE STREET, WILMSLOW.
Wilmslow 3236

Freedom to practise the new morality.

Go-go girls – presumably go-going.

responsibility for the new fashion was the Basque fashion designer André Courrèges, who helped to make the mini-skirt high fashion – and not just in terms of its distance from the ground.

It was the introduction of tights that made the wearing of the mini-skirt a practicable proposition for even the most cowardly of 1960s women. It also had an unexpected effect upon the Inland Revenue. Tax was not levied on children's clothing, and they decided what constituted children's clothing by its length. When they suddenly found a lot of people who were decidedly not children walking around in tax-free clothing, they hurriedly changed their criterion for tax exemption to bust size. Twiggy may still have escaped duty.

Experts offered a variety of explanations for the new fashion: hemlines went up and down with the stock market, said some; others claimed that it was a protest against bourgeois values (Pierre Cardin was one of those who saw clothes as a form of protest); the more practical among them suggested that the mini-skirt provided greater freedom for dancing or practising the new morality. Mary Quant may have been numbered among this last category. When asked by a journalist what the point of fashion was, she replied 'Sex'. (She also claimed that by the 1970s pubic hair would become a focal point of attention for fashion. With

some of the more extreme of her mini-skirts, she was very nearly right.) The mini was not universally loved, any more than it suited everybody. Fashion designer Coco Chanel called it 'the most absurd weapon woman has ever employed to seduce men', and was instrumental in promoting its polar opposite, the trouser suit. These were themselves not without controversy. Some venues barred women wearing them – famously, actress Susannah York was not allowed into New York's Colony restaurant because she was wearing trousers. It was only after fashion icons such as Jackie Kennedy bought trouser suits, from late 1966 onwards, that they became acceptable.

Fashion designers and even retailers were part of the swinging new aristocracy. Mary Quant had traded from her Bazaar store in the Kings Road, Chelsea, since 1955 but it was a run-down back street just off Regent Street that was to become synonymous with 1960s fashion. Carnaby Street was to a significant degree the creation of a Glasgow grocer's son, John Stephen, who opened the first of his ten stores there in 1963. It soon became a tourist mecca, more involved with selling tatty souvenirs to overseas visitors than with serious fashion. The clothes shop became the boutique – by 1967 there were some two thousand establishments in Greater London alone which identified themselves thus.

New materials were much to the fore in the 1960s. Crimplene was introduced in 1961 and plastics, PVC and vinyl were also popular, reflecting – some suggested – the contemporary interest in space exploration. Disposable paper clothes became fashionable, particularly in the United States. American sales of disposable garments in 1967 were estimated at between $50 and $100 millions. It was said that they removed the guilt women felt about buying a dress and wearing it only once or twice. One enterprising sales director had Miss Body Chemistry of 1967 plunging into a heated pool in Baltimore, to demonstrate to the eager press that her paper outfit would not dissolve or shrink. Unfortunately for her, he had not allowed for its tendency to fall off and float away.

Towards the mid-1960s, a more unisex look became

The skirt that became a film.

mary louise ltd ●

BOUTIQUE

UP TO THE MINUTE FASHIONS FOR FASHION MINDED GIRLS, 3-13 years

Mary Louise Girls Fashions are based on Traditional English clothes with a 1968 slant. These are quality tweed trousers and waistcoats, mini-kilts with jackets and Courtauld herring-bone tweed jump-suits. There are also wool dresses with a special plain elegance.

The style illustrated is a lined tweed jacket and trousers to match, and comes in Rust or Grey, sizes 16in. up to 36in. length. The present collection is a budget version of the very expensive range that Mary Louise have made in the past for Prince Rainier's children and the children of H.M. King Hussein.

Shirleys

DEPARTMENT STORE

6 NORTH STREET CHICHESTER

Even the tots had their own boutiques.

*Hairdressers became part of the
decade's fashion aristocracy.*

fashionable, with women wearing
very short hair and both sexes
dressed in hipsters, t-shirts and
skinny rib jumpers. Trouser
bottoms ballooned out and men's
shirt collars and ties became ever
more extravagant. During the latter
years of the decade, the hippie look
arrived. The Afghan coat gave its
wearers the opportunity not only to
look, but also to smell, like a yak,
and the word *casual* ceased to be
adequate to describe young people's
appearance – appallingly scruffy
became the new chic. The mini-
skirt became the micro-skirt and
virtually disappeared from view,
hot pants made their minimal
appearance and the inevitable
reaction, the ankle-length maxi-
skirt, was introduced in 1969.

COMING OUT: THE TOPLESS LOOK

For those at the wild frontiers of fashion, there were topless and
transparent dresses, or ones with bare midriffs and the crocheted see-
through variety. The year 1964 also saw the appearance of the topless
swimsuit. Eastbourne Corporation moved swiftly to ban the latter, under
an Edwardian by-law that imposed a £5 fine for 'indecent exposure of the
female person'. They certainly didn't want anyone frightening the horses
in Eastbourne. The topless fashion never became widespread, but a few
normally demure and retiring young ladies found it necessary to test the
limits of the law's indulgence, usually in the company of a press
photographer. Take, for example, the sisters Valerie and Marion Mitchell,
self-styled cabaret singers. At the London premiere of a film called
London in the Raw (coyly described as 'a production concerned with the
nightlife of the capital'), they turned up unencumbered in the bust
department. It cost them a trip to court and a conditional discharge, which
was small beer compared to the publicity it must have got the film.

Buckinghamshire housewife Mrs Diana Gorton, 27, appeared on
Westminster Bridge during the rush hour and shed her outer garments to
reveal another of the offending dresses. So difficult did she find it to judge
the temperature that she was obliged to put on and take off her outer
garments several times. In doing so, she was evidently oblivious to the cat-
calls from passers-by, but not to the press photographer who just
happened to be passing by at the time. Eventually someone complained to
a policeman, who detained her under an LCC by-law dating from 1900.
Despite protesting her innocence, she received a lecture on morality and
another conditional discharge was issued by the court. But as a

correspondent to *The Times* later pointed out, the nearby statue of Boadicea had been strutting its topless stuff for years and nobody had complained.

Public figures found it necessary to pronounce on the subject of topless dresses. The Archbishop of Canterbury decreed that: 'We must accept the fact that young people express them- selves in new manners of dress that may seem queer to the older of us. We must accept the fact and get alongside them and understand them. A Christian should express his disgust at anything indecent, but short of that, the less disapproval that he* expresses the better.'

More practical advice came from the Guild of Women Motorists, who told us that topless dresses should not be worn while motoring, because they were uncomfortable, impracticable and dangerous, not to mention a distraction to other road users. Members were also told that they would not be acceptable at Guild functions. These pronouncements came from the founder and Secretary of the Guild – inexplicably a Mr Charles Thompson, who was not thought to be personally in any danger of breaching the Guild's dress code.

CLUB CREOLE MEMBERS' NOTICE

REX WILMSLOW

FRIDAY, 8—11 p.m.
ART TAYLOR ALL STARS

SATURDAY, 7.45—11 p.m.
JOHNNY—MIKE and the SHADES

SUNDAY, 7.30—10.30 p.m.
The NASHVILLE MEN
The Tops in Pops

TUESDAY, 8—11 p.m
Another Top-line Beat attraction
FOR ONLY 2/6 SUB.

OVER 18s ONLY — played at every Session by leading Disc-Jockeys.
NO UNCONVENTIONAL DRESS

The Club Creole bans 'unconventional dress' – whatever that meant in the 1960s.

HAIR

One striking symbol of the 1960s abandon was to be seen on the heads of the young – not to mention on those older men who aspired to trendiness and whose follicles were still up to it. Mr Wallace Scowcroft, the President of the National Hairdressers' Federation, summed up the problem from the industry's point of view at their national conference in 1964: 'Men's hairdressers do not object to youth wanting to wear its hair long, provided it is shaped. It would be out of step with modern times to oppose long hair because the hairdresser fears it will lead to fewer visits to his salon. We shall get all the business we want by ensuring that the mods, the rockers and the Beatles fans are well groomed.' However, his tolerance did not extend to 'the slovenly, the dirty and the downright ragged hairdos, of which there are too many about'. He complained of 'beatniks whose hairdos often went with dirty nails, pimples, soiled collars and frayed

*Why did the Archbishop think all the complaints about topless dresses would come from men?

A range of 1960s fashions . . .

It was the age of the mini-skirt . . . though its practicality for country hikes was debatable.

When the minis couldn't get any shorter, they brought in the maxi . . .

. . . and, as the 1960s ended, hot pants started to capture men's undivided attention.

The view from the wild frontiers of 1960s fashion. Even Santa's little helper wasn't immune.

Victims of early 1960s hairdressing.

cuffs. They were symptoms of personal neglect.' He also attacked television actors who 'suffer from the peculiar illusion that those engaged in mass entertainment for ordinary television licence holders like ourselves can appear in front of us wearing feather dusters on their heads instead of hairstyles'.

The audience was foursquare behind the President and, more to the point, voted overwhelmingly in favour of charging long-hairs more for their visits to the hairdresser. But the most famous hair stylist of the decade was Vidal Sassoon. He was born in the East End of London in 1928 and learned his trade under another celebrity crimper, 'Teasy-Weasy' Raymond. He opened up his first salon in 1955 and became a great innovator of hairstyles in the 1960s, creating such masterpieces as the 'One-eyed Girl' look and the Greek Goddess style. One of the later pinnacles of his career was his appointment as hair care consultant to the Los Angeles Olympics in 1984. Such was his success that not a single athlete was forced to retire through dandruff or split ends.

Another hairdresser became famous in the 1960s, but not for his skills with the scissors. When 25-year-old darling of the salons Justin de Villeneuve (better known to his mother as Nigel Davies) started dating a schoolgirl ten years his junior, some might have thought he was moving below his station. The girl concerned, Lesley Hornby, had a 31–22–32 figure that had earned her the nickname 'Sticks' at school. But Villeneuve saw her potential and modified her nickname to 'Twiggy'; he soon became her Svengali and later her fiancé. She became known as London's face of 1966, and before long she was one of the most famous faces in the world. She could earn £80 an hour as a model in New York (at a time when the average wage was only around £15 a week). Twiggy products flooded the market, with the usual beauty and fashion products augmented by the Twiggy lunchbox (these being the days when a lunchbox was simply a box you put your lunch in) as well as ball-point pens, a board game and a Twiggy doll. She retired from modelling in 1969 and went on to careers in acting and pop music.

MODS AND ROCKERS

The Mod cult emerged in the early 1960s, originally as a fashion statement; only later did it degenerate into a licence to commit mayhem on beaches. Mods were characterised by a liking for American R&B, scooters with more chrome than a bathroom showroom, purple hearts (an amphetamine called drynamil) and what passed for snappy dressing in those overwrought years. For the males, this included parkas, hipster trousers, patterned shirts so lurid they had to be viewed through darkened glass, fitted jackets and peaked caps. The female mod was defined by Mary Quant as wearing op-art mini-dresses, PVC 'kinky' boots, coloured tights, soft bras and hair cropped in accordance with the dictates of Vidal Sassoon.

Those Mods who were so inclined found a natural enemy in the Rockers (whose interests may be summarised as Brylcreem, motorcycles, black leather and alcohol). Their battlegrounds were the seaside resorts on Bank Holiday weekends. One such battle took place at Margate over Whitsun weekend in 1964. The fighting started as early as 7 a.m. on the Sunday morning. Windows in the leisure centre and nearby shops were

Diana Dors' husband Alan Lake demonstrates the 1960s male hairstyle.

broken and eleven arrests were made by lunchtime. In the afternoon the participants retired to the beach for further fisticuffs, and the day was rounded off by a hundred Mods, armed with broken bottles and other fashion statements, attacking a group of thirty Rockers. Some four hundred youths were estimated to be involved, fifty-one of whom were arrested. Most were fined (a total of £1,900) but three were sent to prison. The magistrates' outraged rhetoric went into overdrive. Dr George Simpson, Chairman of the Bench, described the participants as 'long-haired, mentally unstable, petty little sawdust Caesars who seem to find courage like rats by hunting in packs'.

Some politicians made rather ill-advised attempts to politicise the disorder. Labour front-bench spokesman Fred Willey said: 'The general complaint of those who took part was that there was nothing for them to do. They came from housing estates with far too few social amenities and were expected to spend their time in amusement arcades . . . the present government regarded working class adolescents as fair game for blatant exploitation by commercial interests.' Strangely enough, the newspapers carried no reports of charities setting up social amenities for these underprivileged and exploited youngsters.

LOVE AND MARRIAGE

The 1960s was allegedly the decade of sexual liberation for women, in which the contraceptive pill became generally available (in January 1961) and family planning became part of the National Health Service (from December of that year). By July 1964 the first family planning clinic catering for unmarried women had opened. The pill was supposed to separate sexual enjoyment from reproduction. But it raised all sorts of other problems, such as leaving women open to emotional blackmail and unhealthy peer group pressures. The health risks connected with taking the pill were also not appreciated at this time.

In 1960 the Marriage Guidance Council launched an initiative for Education in Personal Relationships in schools and youth clubs. The changing moral climate of the day led to more discussion of sexual matters by young people, but in many cases it displayed their appalling ignorance. Schools still tended to limit lessons on reproduction to lower-order species such as amoebas, in case discussion

The pill made it harder for women to resist emotional blackmail and peer group pressures.

of the human variety led to experimentation (this would explain why you found so many pupils behind the school bike sheds, trying unsuccessfully to reproduce by means of binary fission).

The Council tried to teach people not only about the mechanics but also about the associated emotional and moral issues, within a family context. There was a good deal of debate within the organisation as to precisely what, over and above the 'plumbing' matters, could be properly discussed, but the young people set their own agenda. It included contraception, abortion, homosexuality, masturbation (these last two were generally deemed to apply only to boys) and the rules regarding different degrees of petting.

LIBERALISATION OF THE LAW

The 1960s saw important changes in the law which added to Britain's worldwide reputation for progress (or permissiveness, depending on your point of view). The death penalty was suspended on a five-year trial basis in 1965, and on a permanent basis in December 1969, once the trial period had not led to the streets being filled with axe-wielding psychopaths, emboldened by the relaxation in the law. An Abortion Act was steered through Parliament in 1967 at the instigation of former Liberal leader David Steel. The patient still had to obtain a letter from two doctors, saying that the operation was necessary for the physical or psychological well-being of the mother or the family. However, the new law was considerably more liberal (with a small 'l') than the regime that existed in many other countries, and led to a significant – and well-publicised – stream of people coming from abroad to take advantage of it. Under the new law, abortions swiftly rose to more than 130,000 a year – about 10 per cent of the pregnancies conceived within marriage and 35 per cent of those outside.

The Divorce Reform Act of 1969 sought to do away with the concept of having a 'guilty party' in a divorce, and replaced it with 'irretrievable breakdown' of the marriage as the sole criterion. Deliberately indiscreet weekends to Brighton, pursued by a private detective, were no longer required. Irretrievable breakdown was held to mean two years' separation, if both parties consented to the divorce, or five years if they didn't. The law was, however, regarded in some quarters as a 'Casanova's Charter'. It could not be put into practice until further legislation addressed the question of women's rights to property acquired during the course of the marriage. The 1970 Matrimonial Property Act duly established that a wife's work in the home counted equally with paid work outside it when it came to dividing up the goods in the event of a divorce.

There had been pressure to liberalise the law relating to homosexuality since the Wolfenden report had been published in the 1950s. Leo Abse's Bill to remove the worst excesses of the old law was defeated in March 1962. Humphrey Barclay tried to introduce a Bill to decriminalise adult homosexuality in 1966, but it fell again, this time because of that year's General Election. Lord Annan reintroduced it in the Lords in the next session of Parliament and homosexual acts between consenting adults in private were finally decriminalised in 1967.

Deliberately indiscreet weekends to Brighton, pursued by a private detective, were no longer required

DRUGS

The Beatles' album *Sgt Pepper's Lonely Hearts Club Band*, one of the pop icons of the decade, was alleged to feature cannabis plants among the landscaping on its front cover. The lawyers who pored over Peter Blake's photomontage closely enough to make him remove the pictures of Jesus and Gandhi clearly did not have enough expertise in either horticulture or jazz cigarettes to spot them. The Beatles ran into trouble over drugs elsewhere, though, notably in the lavatories of Buckingham Palace while waiting to collect their MBEs, and few other youth cult figures of the decade got away without some brushes with the law over drugs. One of the most famous cases was that of Rolling Stones Keith Richard and Mick Jagger. In early 1967 the *News of the World* published an item on various pop stars' involvement with narcotics. In it they claimed that Mick Jagger had boasted about using LSD and other drugs. Jagger sued the newspaper – they had got the wrong Stone. The one they wanted was the really stoned one, Brian Jones. But these gentlemen of the press were the wrong people to cross in such a way. A few days later, following the receipt of information from somewhere not a million miles from Fleet Street, police raided Keith Richard's Sussex home. They arrested Richard for allowing his house to be used for the consumption of drugs, and Jagger for the possession of some amphetamines which he had obtained perfectly legally in Italy. The court gave them custodial sentences of a year and three months respectively. It became a *cause célèbre*, with *The Times* publishing a famous editorial on the theme of 'Who breaks a butterfly on a wheel?' Pop artist Richard Hamilton produced his picture 'Swingeing London' as a commentary on the case (the judge having spoken of imposing a swingeing sentence as a deterrent to others). On appeal, Richard's conviction was quashed and Jagger got a conditional discharge.

The BBC also took it upon themselves to ban 'A Day in the Life' from the Beatles' *Sgt Pepper* album 'in case it encouraged a permissive attitude to drug taking'. (The song 'I am the Walrus' was similarly banned at about this time, apparently because its use of the word 'knickers' was likely to incite the public to something or other.) The Beatles' own position on drug-taking at this time was ambiguous, to put it mildly. In June 1967 Paul was the first Beatle to admit openly to having used LSD. The following month all four were signatories to a full page advertisement in *The Times* which claimed that 'The law

Wacky baccy was a problem more commonly associated with the youth of the 1960s.

against marijuana is immoral in principle and unworkable in practice'. However, in August of the same year, during their Maharishi Yogi interlude, Paul McCartney announced that the Beatles had renounced drugs, on the grounds that they did not need them any more. (This particular phase lasted about as long as did the Maharishi Yogi in the Beatles' entourage.)

The Beatles' drug career mirrored that of many of the pop nobility of the 1960s. In their early days they were into hard liquor and 'speed' (amphetamines), which kept them going through some of the exhausting touring schedules of that period. They were allegedly introduced to cannabis by Bob Dylan in about the middle of 1964, and at the beginning of the following year John Lennon and George Harrison were given drinks spiked with the drug that became one of the symbols of the decade: LSD.

LSD

Illegal drug manufacturers struggled to keep ahead of the regulators. There were just thirty-three proscribed drugs in Britain in 1950 – but by 1970 the number had risen to 106. One of the most famous of these was a colourless, odourless liquid with a remarkable kick to it. LSD – lysergic acid diethylamide – was first synthesised as long ago as 1938 by the Swiss chemist Dr Albert Hoffman. He was looking for a migraine cure, but what he got instead was a powerful hallucinogen, one that switched off the part of the brain that imposed order on the sensory information coming into it. You were left to cope as best you could with an unedited version of reality. This was seized upon in the early 1960s by West Point drop-out and former army psychologist Dr Timothy Leary, who was sacked from Harvard in 1963 for advocating the use of the drug and, more to the point, for slipping it surreptitiously into the drinks of some of his students. Leary got together with a fellow ex-Harvard colleague, Richard Alpert, and thereafter they became the gurus of LSD and the psychedelic way of life. Leary set up a shop in New York and founded a church, the League of Spiritual Discovery.

The drug was still legal in the United States until 1966, and not difficult to obtain thereafter. Like snake-oil salesmen, Leary and Alpert presented it as a panacea for all the problems of society. According to the hippy-dippythink of the time, the drug helped users to lose their sense of self-importance. By seeing life as a game, they stopped struggling; they became resigned to a pointless, and thus pacific, existence. Bingo! No more war! Unfortunately, this was not the way the drug affected everybody. While some users may well have emerged from their trip crying 'Give peace a chance!', there were plenty who were persuaded by the drug that they could fly off high buildings (which they could, right up to the point where they hit the ground) or worse.

Leary decided to stand for the governorship of California in 1969. The incumbent was an ageing film star with some very firm views on drugs – he himself never used anything stronger than Grecian 2000. His name was Ronald Reagan. Leary asked John Lennon to write an anthem for his campaign – his slogan was going to be 'Come Together'. Whatever the

The law against marijuana is immoral in principle and unworkable in practice

rock and roll merits of the song that Lennon produced, as an election manifesto it was a dubious piece of work. It consisted of a string of apparently unconnected gibberish, though it has to be said that there are some mainstream politicians whose speeches suffer from the same shortcoming (apparently without the assistance of mind-altering drugs). In the event Leary didn't get a chance to test its vote-catching ability. Reagan already had him safely incarcerated in Orange County gaol on a drugs charge, and he made sure that Leary was denied bail for the duration of the election campaign. Only someone far more cynical than I would dare to suggest that Reagan might have used the legal process for political ends.

The group that eventually sprang Leary from prison in 1970 illustrates the darker side of LSD. The Weathermen (later renamed the Weather People in deference to equal opportunities – I kid you not) planted large numbers of bombs at US government facilities between 1969 and 1972. LSD lay at the heart of their view of life, and in order to prevent the CIA from infiltrating their organisation they insisted that everyone attending their meetings had to take LSD at the start. They reasoned that no infiltrator could maintain their cover under its influence. But the darkest manifestation of LSD was the acid fascism practised by Charles Manson and others. Manson used highly effective techniques for brainwashing his followers during their LSD trips, converting them to his murderous manifesto of social and political change, which culminated in the murders at actress Sharon Tate's home.

In order to prevent the CIA from infiltrating their organisation they insisted that everyone attending their meetings had to take LSD at the start

DRUGS – THE OFFICIAL VIEW

It is worth looking at the scale of the official drugs problem in 1960s Britain. Heroin addiction – or at least numbers of registered addicts – increased by about tenfold in the fifteen years between 1953 and 1968. Even so, only 2,782 addicts were registered by 1968. Cannabis started out as a mainly West Indian phenomenon. The first conviction for its use by a teenager was in 1952. There was a rapid escalation in the numbers of cases after about 1965, reaching 2,393 in 1967 and 7,520 by 1970. However, the official statistics remained the tip of a very much bigger iceberg.

Everybody must get peeled
There were plenty of drug rumours about everyday substances that would get you high – things like flower seeds and magic mushrooms. One of the best of these was the story that the scrapings of the inner skin of a ripe banana, dried in an oven and smoked, would get you stoned. The underground press, and then the mainstream papers, latched on to this and the Mellow Yellow Company was set up in San Francisco to develop this new source of intoxication. Even the American Federal Food and Drug Administration claimed to have found that the serotonin in the skins of bananas could be turned by heating into bufotenin, a hallucinogen used by South American Indians. The story turned out to be false, as banana importers breathed a sigh of relief – or possibly cursed their bad luck.

In part this increase in recorded crime in the 1960s may have been explained by the various pieces of legislation tightening drug control. The 1964 Dangerous Drugs Act addressed the use of cannabis, while the 1964 Drugs (Prevention of Misuse) Act tightened controls on amphetamines. It was extended in 1966 to include LSD and other hallucinogens. In 1967 the Dangerous Drugs Act limited the ability of doctors to prescribe drugs to addicts. It also greatly – and controversially – increased police powers to stop and search people for drugs. Baroness Wootton chaired an official enquiry in 1968, which recommended the decriminalisation of cannabis use as a means of breaking the link between soft and hard drugs. They recommended in vain.

CHRONICLE OF THE 1960S: SWINGING BRITAIN – LANDMARKS FOR YOUTH CULTURE

31 December 1960: National Service ends.

30 January 1961: oral contraceptives become available.

11 February 1962: Essex schoolboy sets world record by dancing the twist for thirty-three hours. The world wonders why.

4 November 1963: Beatlemania breaks out at the Royal Variety Show.

13 January 1964: Mary Quant declares Paris fashions out of date.

8 February 1964: the Beatles reach New York.

27 July 1965: the Beatles collect their MBEs.

1 January 1966: Psychedelic Shop opens at Haight Street, San Francisco.

15 January 1966: Trips Festival in San Francisco, held by some to be the start of the hippie movement.

7 October 1966: LSD is declared illegal in California.

14 October 1966: the first edition of the underground newspaper *International Times* was published. Police don't get round to raiding their offices until 9 March 1967.

14 January 1967: first Human Be-In at Golden Gate Park, San Francisco.

30 June 1967: *Sgt Pepper's Lonely Hearts Club Band* released.

August Bank Holiday 1967: Festival of Flower Children at Woburn Abbey.

6 October 1967: 'Death of Hippie' ceremony at Haight Ashbury, just as it is taking off over here.

January 1968: 'Apple' boutique launched by Beatles.

23 January 1969: Proposals to cut penalties for cannabis smoking rejected by the government.

31 August 1969: Isle of Wight Festival, headlined by Bob Dylan, attracts 150,000 fans.

16 September 1969: 'Biba' boutique opens as a department store.

CHAPTER 2

SCANDAL! THE SHOW TRIALS OF THE 1960s

This fictional account of the day-by-day life of an English gamekeeper is still of considerable interest to outdoor minded readers, as it contains many passages on pheasant rearing, the apprehending of poachers, ways to control vermin, and other chores and duties of a professional gamekeeper. Unfortunately, one is obliged to wade through many pages of extraneous material in order to discover and savour these sidelights on the management of a midlands shooting estate, and in this reviewer's opinion this book cannot take the place of J.R. Miller's Practical Gamekeeping.
Alleged review of *Lady Chatterley's Lover* in *Field and Stream*

One of the best illustrations of the clash of the old and new cultures can be seen in the way in which the boundaries of literary taste were tested in the courts during the 1960s. It all started with one of the most famous obscenity trials of all time.

THE NAUGHTY LADY

The obscene publication laws had to be changed at the end of the 1950s since the old Victorian legislation was proving impossible to apply in a changing moral climate. The 1959 Obscene Publications Act required the courts to decide whether a book, taken as a whole, was likely to corrupt or deprave its readers. It allowed as a defence the argument that the standing of the author and the seriousness of his or her intent made publication 'in the interests of science, art, literature or other objects of general concern'. In short, the new law was designed to prevent the prosecution of books like the one that became its first major test case.

Lady Chatterley's Lover by D.H. Lawrence had been banned in England in its unexpurgated form since its first appearance in 1928. For the benefit of anyone who has been living on the moon since 1960, the book concerns the relationship between Lady Chatterley and the family's gamekeeper, Mellors. When Lady Chatterley's husband returns from the First World War paralysed from the waist down and generally in less than full working order in the marital bliss department, Mellors takes on what the expurgated version might have referred to as 'certain other duties around the estate'. The book is a frank and explicit account of their passionate relationship, with all sorts of allegorical overtones about the class system.

Courts in other countries had taken differing views on the book. In Canada it was banned, but in the USA it was not considered obscene and could be sent legally through the mail (to Canada, for example?). In August 1961 Penguin Books, emboldened by the new law, announced their plan to publish an unexpurgated version of the novel in Britain. One of the first applications for a copy came from that well-known seat of literary criticism, New Scotland Yard. Copies were duly dispatched to them and this was deemed to constitute publication, even though the book never went on sale officially anywhere.

A prosecution under the 1959 Obscene Publications Act followed, and both sides scurried around looking for witnesses to speak for or against the book's literary merits. The defence side had an embarrassment of riches, from the Bishop of Woolwich to a newly graduated English literature student, with many of the great and the good of the literary establishment in between. The prosecution failed to find anyone of stature (they had apparently tried unsuccessfully to get T.S. Eliot). They were thus unable to present any evidence and were reduced to trying to knock holes in the defence case.

Enter the prosecuting counsel, one of the most remarkable legal minds of the 1960s. Mr Mervyn Griffith-Jones QC was to be found on the prosecution side of many of the famous trials of the 1960s, especially those involving any sexual scandal. He earned himself a place in legal history at this trial by asking the jury whether *Lady Chatterley* was a book you would want your wife or your servants to read. This Welsh nonconformist eventually ceased practising as a barrister, taking up a position where lack of touch with reality would be no impediment – he became a judge.

The defence started to work through the seventy-one or so witnesses who all wanted to speak in favour of the book. The Bishop of Woolwich said it was a book all Christians might read with profit, and likened the sexual act to a form of holy communion. This upset a number of Christians, from the Archbishop of Canterbury down. The Bishop seems to have developed a taste for controversy, since he went on in 1963 to publish *Honest to God*, a bestselling reinterpretation of the Christian faith that many saw as deeply sacrilegious and even as the starting point for much of the moral decline of the decade.

Batting for the Catholic branch of the church was the barrister Norman St John Stevas, author of that essential volume *Obscenity and the Law*. He said that every Catholic, including priests, should read *Lady Chatterley*, since its aim was to rid sexual activity of false shame. He told the court how he had had the 'misfortune' to study a great deal of pornography in the course of researching his book. *Lady Chatterley* had nothing in common with them and D.H. Lawrence was, in his view, one of the great moralists of the century.

Mellors takes on what the expurgated version might have referred to as 'certain other duties around the estate'

D.H. Lawrence. The man was an obvious deviant – why, he even had a beard!

As the parade of witnesses went on, prosecuting counsel did his best to undermine the reputations of both D.H. Lawrence and Lady Constance Chatterley. It became difficult at times to remember that this was not a divorce case, citing her adultery as the shameful grounds. Ignoring the law's requirement that you should look at the work as a whole, Griffith-Jones read out selected passages to the witnesses, and asked them whether they thought it was either well written or moral. He seemed to have a fixation about the number of times words like bowels or womb appeared on the page, and whether this undermined its literary or moral worth.

Nothing was too peripheral to add weight to his case. He threw in the fact that Lawrence was himself an adulterer in real life (notwithstanding the fact that he eventually married the woman concerned – Frieda von Richthofen, cousin of the German aviator – and remained with her for the rest of his life). He pointed out that Lady Chatterley and Mellors never had any proper conversations during the course of their sexual activity (in which case, about 99 per cent of the population were guilty of whatever it was he was trying to prove). He argued that Lawrence's misquotation at one point from the Book of Psalms undermined his worth as an author. He even tried to produce a volume of crime statistics to suggest that D.H. Lawrence's as-yet-unpublished book was responsible for the crime wave, arguing that: 'One only has to read one's daily papers to see the kind of thing that is happening. It is all through lack of standards, lack of restraint, lack of mental and moral discipline.' It was all, he said, due to the influences that the younger generation were open to – the Sunday papers, the cinemas and literature. From there, he moved on to the allegorical content of the book, asking the jury whether they thought the girls in the factory (and, presumably, their servants) would see a particular episode in the book at the allegorical level:

I submit to you that the tendency of that passage can only be to raise impure and lustful thoughts in the minds of some, indeed many, who will read this book. . . . You would have to go some way in the Charing Cross Road, the back streets of Paris and even Port Said to find a description of sexual intercourse that was perhaps as lurid as that.

The defence, for its part, argued that: 'There are minds which are unable to see beauty where it exists and doubt the integrity of purpose in an author where it is obvious.' No doubt, they suggested, in whatever murky processes were going on in Mr Griffith-Jones' mind, Shakespeare's *Antony and Cleopatra* was just a play about adultery – a sex-starved man copulating with an Egyptian Queen.

By half way through the long parade of witnesses, the entire court was losing the will to live. Even the prosecution could not find any new lines of cross-examination and not all those who wanted to testify actually got to speak. During the summing up, even Mr Griffith-Jones had to acknowledge that Lawrence was a writer of some standing and honesty of purpose, and that the offending work itself had *some* literary merit. The judge in his summing up tried to drag the jury back to the provisions of the law, asking them to consider the book as a whole – they were not a board of censors with blue pencils. He did, however, mention that the proposed selling price of the book – *3s 6d* – would bring it within the reach of the vast mass of the population, raising some quaintly paternalistic nineteenth-century concerns as to whether this was the sort of stuff you could safely allow the working classes to read.

The jury had no difficulty deciding. In just three hours they returned a verdict of not guilty, which was greeted by applause in the court. Of course, all the publicity surrounding the trial had precisely the effect the book's opponents did not want. On its first day on sale, the entire edition of 200,000 copies was snapped up and the book's sales went on to exceed four million.

The arguments continued in the newspaper letter pages after the trial was over, and the correspondents proved even more inventive than Mr Griffith-Jones. One, a former policeman turned vicar, opposed the book on the grounds that the inevitable consequence of adulterous relationships was illegitimate children and, as everybody knew, illegitimate children were 'crime-prone'. Another pointed out that there was not equal freedom in different media. Had D.H. Lawrence tried to portray in pictures what he said in words, he would most undoubtedly have been prosecuted. (*The Illustrated Lady Chatterley's Lover*? The mind boggles! If that ever gets published, surely the pop-up book cannot be far behind?)

Had D.H. Lawrence tried to portray in pictures what he said in words, he would most undoubtedly have been prosecuted

OTHER SHOW TRIALS OF THE 1960S

There were further high-profile obscenity trials during the 1960s, as the boundaries of the law were stretched to their limits. Mr Griffith-Jones was to have more luck prosecuting the case of *Fanny Hill*, John Cleland's rather more obviously titillating book about an eighteenth-century woman of pleasure. Alexander Trocchi's work *Cain's Book* established in 1964 that obscenity was not limited to matters sexual, when Lord Chief Justice

Parker ruled that a book which appeared to advocate drug-taking was depraved and obscene. In some cases it appeared that the lifestyles of the authors were on trial as much as the subject matter of their literature.

One case in which literary merit played no part whatsoever was that of Frederick Shaw and his work *The Ladies' Directory*. For two shillings this supplied the reader with details of all London's ladies of easy virtue and the specialised services they offered (with the words *corr.* indicating strict disciplinarians and *full wardrobe* that they were willing to dress up as 'Nanny Leatherstockings' or whatever else took their clients' bizarre fancies). In Shaw's case, an obscene publication conviction was compounded with living off immoral earnings and conspiring to corrupt the public morals.

The trial of *Last Exit to Brooklyn* was most notable for the appearance of Robert Maxwell on the prosecution side, denouncing the book's publishers as being motivated purely by money. This was a private prosecution bought by an antediluvian Eastbourne MP, Sir Charles Taylor, who seemed more likely to take a cup of cocoa to bed than a book like this. None the less he managed to get the Reverend David Shepherd to condemn it and bookseller Sir Basil Blackwell to admit that he himself had been depraved by the book. But not even these star witnesses could prevent the eventual publication of the book.

The changing moral climate was also reflected in the cinema.

By the end of the decade, the boundaries of the permissible had been extended considerably. Books like Philip Roth's *Portnoy's Complaint* (largely devoted to what used to be referred to as 'the solitary vice') and *The Naked Lunch* (the violent homo-erotic ravings of former heroin addict William Burroughs) were being published without challenge. Whether it was also without cost to society is a matter for speculation. When Lord Longford chaired a committee in the early 1970s to investigate the growth of hard-core pornography – which nobody pretended had any redeeming literary merits – they found that the number of publications impounded in 1972 exceeded 2,500,000: fifty times the number confiscated in 1960. The incidence of rape and other sexual offences also rose five-fold between 1950 and 1975, though whether this was linked to the liberalisation of censorship is another debate which goes well beyond the scope of this book.

THE LORD CHAMBERLAIN'S PEN

The law relating to the theatre was also liberalised. Hitherto, the Lord Chamberlain – a member of the Royal Household – had the power of veto over theatrical productions before they were performed. This situation had applied for some four hundred years. The veto was applied originally through the use of the Royal Prerogative, until in 1737 Sir Robert Walpole passed a law to prevent satirists saying horrible things about him and his government. The main target of the new law was John Gay and his *Beggar's Opera*, and the success of the legislation may be judged from the fact that the *Beggar's Opera* was enjoying yet another revival on the London stage at just about the time the Lord Chamberlain's powers were finally being repealed.

Efforts had been made to review the system from as long ago as 1909, but the Lord Chamberlain showed no signs of wishing to join the twentieth century. No playwright was too elevated to be safe from him – works by Shaw, Ibsen and Pirandello were all censored – and no expletive too mild to escape his pen. One attempt at gritty realism had every 'bloody' struck from the script. It was the 1950s before any serious reference to homosexuality was allowed on the stage. The operation of this law began to look increasingly ludicrous by the 1960s. The Lord Chamberlain banned the performance on stage of a sketch already shown on television's *That Was The Week That Was* (the one about the sinking of the Royal Barge – see page 72). Thus a few hundred people were prevented from seeing what millions had already seen, apparently without any major collapse of public order.

In Spike Milligan's *The Bed Sitting Room* there was a spoof advertisement for Daz, 'getting all the dirt off the tail of your shirt'. The Lord Chamberlain insisted that this be changed to 'off the front of your shirt' (which some felt to be even ruder). Other changes were simply incomprehensible to author and audience alike. There was a feeling that someone very officious, or very sick, was exercising these powers. From 1966 onwards moves were made to put theatre on an equal footing with literature. This culminated in the Theatres Act of 1968, abolishing the Lord Chamberlain's powers and making the theatre subject to tests of obscenity similar to those endured by book publishers.

There was a feeling that someone very officious, or very sick, was exercising these powers

HAIR

The very day after this Act became law, the show *Hair* opened in London. It was described as a 'tribal love-rock musical' and had been created by two New York actors who were apparently inspired by a Flower People's anti-Vietnam 'be-in' in Central Park. It used nudity and four-letter words to celebrate the evasion of the draft – a combination clearly designed to win the hearts and minds of middle England. At the climax of the show, the naked cast joined hands and sang. One of the more cherishable moments in the production came at this point in the show when, one night, a female member of the cast reached out to grasp her neighbour's hand but instead seized another part of him. (I trust I do not need to paint a picture.)

Like the satire movement, discussed later, the Establishment took *Hair* to its ample bosom and absorbed it. At the end of the show the audience were invited to defy theatrical convention and join the cast, dancing on stage. On the first night, the audience's charge on to the stage was led by those well-known anti-Establishment figures, the Duke of Bedford and Zsa Zsa Gabor. We knew that *Hair* had finally failed in its subversive purpose when Princess Anne not only went to see it, but got up on the stage and danced with the rest of the audience at the end. Even the theatre critic of *The Times* loved it: 'Nothing else remotely like it has yet struck the West End. As a musical, it is utterly remote from the values and formulae of orthodox show business. . . . its honesty and passion give it the quality of a true theatrical celebration – the joyous sound of a group of people telling the world exactly what they feel.'

PUSHING THE BOUNDARIES

Other productions previously considered 'beyond the pale' were being lined up for the London stage at the same time. Kenneth Tynan, who had already earned the dubious distinction of being the first man to use the dreaded F-word on television, brought his production of *Oh, Calcutta!* to London. It was described by the *New York Times* drama critic as the kind of show that gave pornography a bad name, and was only staged after the Attorney General gave an assurance that he would not prosecute. It naturally enjoyed great commercial success, but it led Sir Alan Herbert, one of the original champions of the liberalisation of the obscenity laws, to lament that: 'The worthy struggle for reasonable liberty for honest writers has ended in a right to represent copulation, veraciously, on the public stage.'

There were always those who wanted to test the law to its limits. Hermann Nitsch's 'event' *Abreaktionspiel*, staged at the St Bride's Institute, was one such. In this, the carcass of a lamb was subjected to various indignities before being ripped asunder. The unfortunate creature's entrails were then emptied into the trousers of one of the cast, who extracted them through his fly. The remains of the lamb were next covered with simulated blood and a film projected on to it. The film showed a penis, attached to a piece of string, being manipulated (rather like a puppet version of 'Viagra – the Movie'). The police officers present failed to appreciate the deep artistic significance of this sensitive work and the organisers were fined £100 for putting on 'an exhibition of a lewd, indecent and disgusting nature'. Andrew Lloyd-Webber's musical version is awaited with interest.

The police announced that they were reviewing their staffing situation in the light of the new laws. They did not intend, they said, to send an officer to every first night performance. They preferred to rely on complaints from members of the public to find out where the really interesting stuff was going on.

Somebody who was trying to push the standards of public morality back in the other direction was 'Mary, Mary, Quite Contrary'.* Early

*The title of her autobiography.

in the 1960s the Head of the Art Department was summoned to see the head teacher at Madeley Secondary Modern School in Shropshire. She was asked to take charge of the moral welfare of the girls, which included the dispensing of sex education. This was to be based on the principles of the recently published Newsom Report on Secondary Education, which preached 'chastity before marriage and fidelity within it'.

During one of her sex education lectures, she was surprised to see one of her pupils fall off her chair in a dead faint. It turned out that she had witnessed sex-related violence between her parents. It brought home to the teacher the differing susceptibilities of young people to the messages they received about sex through the media. Increasingly, it seemed to her, people were being engulfed in a wave of licentiousness and immorality. As she put it: 'Homosexuality, prostitution and sexual intercourse became the routine accompaniment of the evening meal.'

In case you were wondering whether how she fitted all this in as well as marking the homework, she was referring to the programmes on her television. The problem ranged from the smutty and disrespectful satire of *That Was The Week That Was*, through the coverage of the Profumo scandal and the fictional output of the media, with all the unspeakable things going on around the kitchen sink; to the permissive advice being dispensed to teenagers and even the BBC's 'South Bank' approach to religious broadcasting during the era of *Honest to God*.

By May 1964 she and three others decided to do something about it. They had two thousand copies of a petition printed and, having no idea how to promote it, wrote a letter to the *Birmingham Evening Post*. It was the *Post*'s reporter who persuaded them to organise a public meeting in Birmingham Town Hall. She duly booked it, blissfully unaware that it seated 2,000 people. Once she realised the scale of the commitment she was panic-stricken, and hoped desperately that at least a couple of hundred people would turn up to fill a corner of the hall. She need not have worried, for her crusade had struck a deep chord in a section of the British public. The town hall was packed. Thirty-nine coachloads arrived, from as far away as Devon and Scotland, and a group of what she described as 'long-haired students' rushed the stage and tried to take

The one sure way to get tickets for the best first nights – join the police.

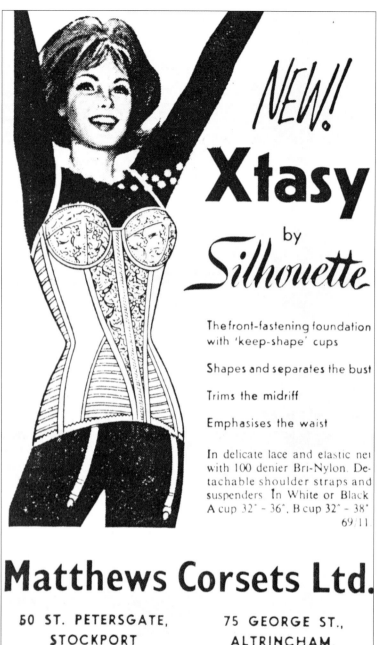

NEW!

Xtasy

by

Silhouette

The front-fastening foundation with 'keep-shape' cups

Shapes and separates the bust

Trims the midriff

Emphasises the waist

In delicate lace and elastic net with 100 denier Bri-Nylon. Detachable shoulder straps and suspenders. In White or Black A cup 32˝ – 36˝. B cup 32˝ – 38˝ 69/11.

Matthews Corsets Ltd.

50 ST. PETERSGATE, STOCKPORT

75 GEORGE ST., ALTRINCHAM.

102 WATER LANE, WILMSLOW

SPECIALISTS IN CORSETRY

1960s body armour – designed to ward off the most ardent youth. Mrs Whitehouse would no doubt approve.

control of the microphone. One good handbagging later, order was restored, the 'Clean Up TV Campaign' was well and truly born, and Mary Whitehouse (for it was she) had become a national figure. Naturally, the BBC transmitted only scenes of the attempted disruption of the meeting.

The campaign got off to the most dramatic start. Church leaders, from the Archbishop of Canterbury downwards, lent their support and the doors of senior media figures were opened to the campaigners – some, such as that of the Director-General of the BBC, Hugh Carlton-Greene, with the greatest reluctance. The campaign targeted the BBC because it was felt that, as it was a public corporation, the public should have some say in its output. It might also have had something to do with Greene's attitude towards the campaign, which was much less sympathetic than that of the more emollient Lord Hill (the former TV Doctor and Chairman of the Independent Television Authority).

Television progressives fought back – notably with the television series *Swizzlewick*, in which a thinly disguised Mrs Smallgood launched a 'Freedom from Sex' campaign, featuring characters based on many of the leading lights of the National Listeners & Viewers' Association. Mrs Whitehouse described the programme thus: 'This skit, which showed councillors to be stupid and corrupt, [was] a gross insult to public-spirited men giving freely of their time; parents were furious that family viewing time should be taken up with what the *Catholic Pictorial* described as "obscene offerings of adolescent smut"; and television critics could find little to praise.'

A more direct acknowledgement of her impact on the public consciousness was to come in the 1990s, when a comedy team that could hardly be said to represent the values she held most dear chose to name themselves 'The Mary Whitehouse Experience'. Vilification, not imitation, is the sincerest form of flattery.

Her task was made easier (and Hugh Greene's impossible) when Harold Wilson made Lord Hill Chairman of the Governors of the BBC in 1967. By the end of the decade, Mary's Association had become a powerful pressure group against the prevailing trend towards the liberalisation of the media. She would go on to be a leading figure in the Festival of Light of the 1970s, in the prosecution of *Gay News* under the Blasphemy Act, and in the campaign for a Broadcasting Standards Council, which bore fruit in 1991.

CHRONICLE OF THE 1960S: THE LAW

19 September 1960: The 1960 Road Traffic Act leads to the City of Westminster introducing the first traffic wardens. The first ticket is awarded to a doctor who was in the middle of treating a patient who had suffered a heart attack.

The traffic warden – fearless custodian of the parking laws – treats rich and poor alike.

1 May 1961: The Betting and Gaming Act leads to the first legal betting shops. Their advertising is so strictly controlled that they prove hard for people to find.

1961: The Identikit comes into use by the police. A Mr Edwin Bush becomes the first criminal to be caught with its help.

3 June 1962: Britain's first legal casino opens in Brighton.

20 June 1966: The first 'coloured' policeman – Kenyan-born Mohamet Yusuf Daar – becomes PC492 with Coventry police force.

5 October 1967: Juries are allowed to reach majority verdicts for the first time. The first person to be sentenced through this process is a Mr Saleh Kassem, a professional wrestler whose ring name is 'The Terrible Turk'. He is convicted of stealing a handbag.

1 January 1968: The first black woman – Mrs Sislin Fay Allen from Jamaica – begins training as a WPC.

CHAPTER 3

BETRAYAL: 1960s ESPIONAGE

I have no reason to conclude that Mr Philby has at any time betrayed the interests of this country.
Harold Macmillan, Foreign Secretary, addressing the Commons in 1955 (four years after the CIA told us that Philby was spying for Russia)

The spy story became one of the favourite film and book themes of the 1960s. No doubt this was fuelled by the amount of real-life espionage that was in the news at the time. Unfortunately, most of it seemed to involve people spying for the Communists against the west, and it highlighted the incompetence of our intelligence services in their efforts to catch them.

THE PORTLAND RING

This sorry saga began in January 1961, when five people were arrested. Two of them – Henry Houghton and Ethel Gee – were Admiralty civil servants at the Underwater Weapons Establishment at Portland. Houghton had developed a taste for expensive nightlife and women during a posting to Warsaw and the Russian government had thoughtfully subsidised it on his return to Britain. Two of the others – Peter and Helen Kroger – were living in a bungalow in Ruislip and running an antiquarian book business on the Strand. But their New Zealand passports were false. They had obtained them by having some out-of-date passports forged and then posting them back to the New Zealand government for renewal. They were really American citizens by the name of Cohen, who had fled to Britain from New York after the exposure of the Rosenberg spy ring. The Krogers' small suburban house contained all the makings of 'a thriller' – as the trial judge himself was later to observe. There was a high-powered radio transmitter, microdots, cigarette lighters and torches with false compartments; miniature cameras, letters in Russian and secret naval documents, containing details of anti-submarine devices and fleet orders.

Their leader was someone calling himself Gordon Lonsdale. He posed as a Canadian businessman but he was really a Russian citizen, a KGB agent called Kolon Molodi. He claimed to have been educated in California, but there was no record of his existence there before 1955, at which time he would have been about thirty. He was the son of a Russian scientist, who was smuggled into Canada aged about eleven. It was possible even then that he was intended to be a 'sleeper' – an agent who would lie dormant for a long period. He returned to Russia during the Second World War and, aged seventeen, was dropped behind the German lines to spy for his native country. Eventually, he found his way to England, where he ran a company selling, among other things, bubble-gum machines and juke-boxes. But his real interest lay in the nuclear submarine base at Holy Loch – which became an unexpectedly attractive market for his bubble-gum machines.

At the trial, all five pleaded not guilty, but they received sentences of between fifteen and (in Lonsdale's case) twenty-five years. The best that Lonsdale's counsel could offer in mitigation was that 'at least he was not a traitor to his country'. However, Lonsdale did not serve much of his sentence – he was 'swapped' in April 1964 for the British 'businessman' Greville Wynne (this is one of those irregular declensions. It goes 'Our man is a businessman, yours is a spy, theirs is a traitor'.) Lonsdale/Molodi died in mysterious circumstances near Moscow in 1970. The Krogers were also exchanged – this time in 1969 for Gerald Brooke, a lecturer imprisoned by the Russians for handing out subversive literature.

At least he was not a traitor to his country

BLAKE'S FORTY-TWO

Lonsdale was said to be a professional spy, doing it for the money. George Blake, who was tried in May 1961, betrayed his country for ideological reasons. He was born George Behar in Rotterdam in 1922, the son of a Jew from Constantinople who had acquired British citizenship by fighting for our side during the First World War. Blake inherited his father's citizenship without either of them ever having set foot in Britain. When the Second World War broke out, Blake escaped from Holland disguised as a Trappist monk. He made his way to England and, like his father, volunteered to fight for the allies. He was enrolled in the Navy and spent the war working with spies going into Holland. The security service took him on after the war, fondly assuming that his wartime record was proof enough of his loyalty. But, as Blake was later to put it: 'My loyalty was to the anti-Nazi cause, not to Britain.'

He took a course in Russian at Cambridge and was posted to the British Embassy in Seoul in 1948 as Vice-consul, where his job was to set up intelligence sources at the Russian port of Vladivostok, some 450 miles away. His task proved impossible, since communications between the two places were virtually non-existent, and his failure was criticised by his superiors. Then the Korean War broke out and Blake was captured by the advancing North Korean forces in June 1950. During his captivity, the story goes, he read *Das Kapital*, came to the conclusion that he was working for the wrong side and the Russians then coached him to spy for them. The Koreans held him until April 1953, after which he returned 'home', something of a hero to his fellow SIS (Secret Intelligence Service) officers. Despite his rather unusual career path, he was given only a cursory two-hour debriefing by the authorities, who once again took his loyalty for granted. Nobody thought that country bumpkins like the Koreans would be capable of 'turning' one of our chaps.

In fact it is quite possible that the story about him being turned was invented by British intelligence to hide their embarrassment at the fact that Blake had been a spy in their midst for years. Whatever the truth, within six weeks George Blake was in contact with his Soviet controller in London. He was posted to Berlin and given the job of recruiting Soviet staff and KGB officers to the allied cause, and of gathering information that could be used to blackmail those who did not come over voluntarily. Between then and 1959, he betrayed every one of the four hundred or so people in the SIS's German operation to the Russians. His employers thoughtfully gave him free run of a card index on which all their names were kept, to make his job easier. His treachery cost the lives of some forty people, a fact which was later passed on surreptitiously to his trial judge.

In 1959 he was posted back to London to recruit British businessmen, students and tourists visiting Russia as spies, and to turn Russians resident in Britain, plant interpreters and bug buildings. It was while he was on a course to learn Arabic in Beirut that evidence of his other activities came to light. He was brought home and after three days' cross-examination began pouring out a catalogue of betrayal that left his interrogators slack-jawed with amazement. At one point, he interrupted his monologue to ask: 'Am I boring you?'

Not in the least, they assured him. He then asked for a revolver and some time alone in the room, a request which was denied. It's not as serious as that, his interrogators falsely assured him. At this point lawyers told them that Blake's confession was worthless, since he had not been cautioned. If he were to revoke it later, a trial judge might throw the case out. Blake was duly issued with a tame solicitor, one who could be relied upon to forget about his duty to serve his client's interests, and who would persuade him to sign a confession and plead guilty.

Prime Minister Macmillan was none too pleased at the news of Blake's arrest. 'The government could fall over this' he told the security service, and suggested that Blake be given immunity, despite his appalling record. Macmillan was only eventually persuaded to allow the trial to go ahead provided the Attorney General found some way to ensure that Blake got more than the normal fourteen years maximum sentence for such offences. Blake duly signed his confession, in the fond belief that he would be out in fourteen years, less remission.

Most of the case was conducted in secret, for reasons of national security, in front of Lord Chief Justice Parker. The public of the day learned tantalisingly little about the man and his crimes. When it was time for sentencing, the judge stunned the court and, more particularly, the defendant. He gave Blake the maximum fourteen-year sentence for each of the five charges against him, but ruled that three of them should be served consecutively, giving him a sentence of forty-two years, with not even a hope of parole until twenty-eight years had been served. It was the longest sentence ever handed out in a British court.

His treachery cost the lives of some forty people

Harold Macmillan, who was not at all pleased about the arrest of the spy George Blake.

Blake did not wait around. He proved such a model prisoner at Wormwood Scrubs that the prison authorities disregarded SIS warnings that he would try to escape. On the contrary, they granted him extra privileges, such as exercising in an area right next to the outer walls. His escape did not require the resources of the KGB, just the help of a fellow prisoner. The man concerned was a disaffected Irishman called Sean Bourke. Bourke befriended Blake in prison, regarding him as a prisoner of conscience. On his own release, Bourke vowed to help Blake get away. Somehow he smuggled into the prison a complete escape outfit, including a walkie talkie (over which he and Blake talked for anything up to two hours at a time, without detection), a camera (for arranging passport photographs), a car jack (for bending the bars of his cell), wire cutters, three lengths of clothes line and thirty steel knitting needles (for fashioning a ladder). Equally amazing, Blake managed to conceal it all in the prison.

On 22 October 1966 Blake climbed to freedom. He broke his wrist in a fall on the other side and holed up in a flat close to the prison until mid-December. A camper van with a hidden compartment then provided the means for him to cross the Channel and make his way to East Germany. Blake later turned up in Moscow, where he received the Order of Lenin.

WILLIAM VASSALL

It was in October 1962 that career civil servant William John Vassall was brought to trial. He was sentenced at the very height of the Cold War, the week before the news of the Cuban missile crisis broke. His was one of the best known, but certainly not the first, cases of someone being forced to spy as a result of entrapment. Vassall had been posted to the Naval Attaché's office at the British Embassy in Moscow in March 1954. A practising homosexual (in fact, he was said to practise so much he must have perfected it), he struck up a relationship in the Embassy with a Pole named Mikhailski. Mikhailski took him to a friend's house for a meal. Having plied him with food and strong drink, his new friends remarked on how hot it was, and helped Vassall off with his jacket. The heat may have had something to do with the strong lighting in the room. Vassall's suspicions should have been aroused when they helped him off with all his other clothes as well. But it was only when some secret police officers showed up later with some highly incriminating photographs showing Vassall waving his underpants around his head, that the extent of his problems became clear. They told him that he could be imprisoned in Russia for what he had been up to, unless he co-operated with them. Vassall had been the victim of a classic 'honeypot' operation, set up by General Oleg Gribanov of Russian intelligence, who specialised in such arrangements.

From that point onwards Vassall started to spy for the Russians, and he continued to do so on his return to Britain in 1956. The Russians gave him a miniature camera and made payments to him that roughly doubled his income (of about £980 a year, gross). He contacted his minders in the best James Bond fashion, by drawing a circle in pink chalk around certain trees in a London park or by ringing a Kensington number and asking for 'Miss Mary'. The authorities might have been suspicious of an overtly homosexual man (it was illegal at that time, and he was known to his colleagues at work as 'Auntie'), who had access to secret documents, and who was living in a flat in Dolphin Square which should have been well beyond his means. But it was September 1962 before he was finally uncovered, when KGB officer Anatoli Golitsin defected to the CIA and began naming KGB informants.

Prime Minister Macmillan understated the case when he said that he was 'not at all pleased' at this latest failure of security, or the arrest which followed. He went on: 'When my gamekeeper shoots a fox, he doesn't go and hang it up outside the Master of Foxhounds' drawing room; he buries it out of sight. But you can't just shoot a spy, as you did in the war. You have to try him. . . . Better to discover him, and then control him, but never catch him.'

Vassall got eighteen years for his espionage. There were press allegations of a cover-up and stories of some kind of improper relationship with a junior minister began to emerge. Vassall worked for Thomas Galbraith, a former Civil Lord at the Admiralty, the Conservative Member of Parliament for one of the Glasgow constituencies and son of the peer Lord Strathclyde. Among his other tasks, Vassall used to ferry top secret documents to Galbraith at his

But you can't just shoot a spy, as you did in the war. You have to try him. . . . Better to discover him, and then control him, but never catch him

Scottish home. Galbraith knew Vassall well enough to describe him, during his rather inept defence of his own innocence, as 'having a screw loose'. This simply begged the question as to why he entrusted top secret documents to him. After Galbraith moved to the Scottish Office, Vassall had kept in touch with his former boss, sending him ingratiating letters, to which Galbraith foolishly replied.

Vassall was later to sell his correspondence with Galbraith to the *Sunday Pictorial* for £5,000. Rumours began to circulate of 'perverted and immoral behaviour', and of plans for the two of them to defect. The *Pictorial* sent copies of the correspondence to the government, but also copied them to the leader of the opposition. Matters came to a head when the full text of the correspondence was published in the press. In fact it showed evidence of nothing more damning than mind-numbing banality, dealing at one point with Galbraith's need for a supply of small bulldog clips. If Galbraith could be accused of anything, it was of showing bad judgement in being rather too accommodating towards a pushy junior member of staff. Sir Charles Cunningham conducted an inquiry into the security aspects of the case. He found 'no prima facie evidence of a security risk' but Galbraith felt it necessary to resign for the embarrassment he had caused the government. Galbraith's career never really recovered from this setback. He later served a further spell as a junior minister but died, a back-bench Member of Parliament, in 1982. Vassall, meanwhile, was released from prison in 1972, and published his memoirs in 1975. The Vassall case further reinforced the view that there was something seriously wrong with British security. It would not be long before doubters were given further ammunition.

THE THIRD MAN

Harold 'Kim' Philby was the son of a famously eccentric explorer, Harry Philby, who acted as an advisor to many Middle Eastern governments. Kim (nicknamed after the Rudyard Kipling story) was educated at Westminster and then at Cambridge, which at that time was producing almost more spies than future Members of Parliament (among the other Cambridge alumni of that period were Burgess, Maclean and Blunt). While at Cambridge he joined an elite group known as the Apostles, which was used by the Russians as a recruiting ground for espionage agents. He also became a Communist, and was married at one time to an Austrian Communist, Litzi Friedmann, who herself turned out to be a Soviet agent. All that was missing was an out-tray on his desk, marked 'Secrets for Moscow' in big letters.

But none of this impeded his progress in the civil service. They may have been influenced by the fact that, in addition to his Communist leanings, he was also at one time a member of the Anglo-German Fellowship, a pro-Nazi group. While Philby may well have enrolled in this as a blind at the suggestion of his Russian masters, the internal contradictions in his allegiances might well have made

Cambridge at that time was producing almost more spies than future Members of Parliament

The internal contradictions in his allegiances might well have made him appear a crackpot to many people

him appear a crackpot to many people. To British intelligence, they apparently just made him a well-rounded individual, since MI6 not only recruited him – but went on to make him their Deputy Head and prospective Head.

After the war, he had an early opportunity to apply his skills. The Soviet diplomat Constantin Volkhov approached the British Embassy in Istanbul with an offer to defect, promising in return to name three Russian moles in British intelligence. Philby, who was certainly one of the three, volunteered to go to Istanbul and investigate. On his way, he tipped off the Russians. Philby delayed his arrival long enough for a heavily bandaged Mr Volkhov to be transported rather swiftly back to Russia, where the error of his ways was no doubt firmly pointed out to him.

Philby, meanwhile, became First Secretary of the British Embassy in Washington, where he worked closely with the CIA. This position enabled him in 1951 to tip off fellow spies Burgess and Maclean that the authorities were on to them, thus allowing them to escape to Russia. From as early as 1951 MI5 suspected him of being a spy (not least because the American intelligence service had told them he was) but he was protected by the mutual antipathy between MI5 and MI6, in which Philby served. This hostility was intrinsic to the different roles they performed. MI5 is basically a defensive operation, whose job is catching and locking up spies. MI5's instinct is always to close breaches in security when they are discovered, even if it means telling the other side that their agent has been uncovered. MI6 exists to gather secret information in clandestine ways. Their preferred option is to keep an enemy agent operating, in order to obtain further information. In Philby's case, MI6 'regarded the MI5 suspicion as quite unjustified and essentially an expression of MI5's overall distrust of its sister service'. 'Lord help the sister who comes between me and my man', as the Beverley Sisters were to put it, in another context. MI5 insisted on Philby being given a secret 'trial' in 1951. The results were inconclusive, though Philby left the Diplomatic Service, pocketing a £3,000 gratuity from public funds for his trouble as he did so. But MI6 continued to operate him, even assisting later in his transfer to the Middle East, a move which was to aid his eventual defection.

Although Burgess and Maclean defected in May 1951 their status as Soviet spies was not officially confirmed until 1955, when the Russian diplomat Vladimir Petrov fled to Australia and started telling the world about his former employer's intelligence operations. The House of Commons debated the defection of Burgess and Maclean in November 1955 and Philby's alleged involvement was already being talked about. In his speech to the House, Harold Macmillan (then Foreign Secretary) displayed the fine judgement of character that was to stand him in such good stead in the Profumo case: 'No evidence has been found to show that [Philby] was responsible for warning Burgess and Maclean. While in government service he carried out his duties ably and conscientiously. I have no reason to conclude that Mr Philby has at any time betrayed the interests of this country, or to identify him with the so-called "third man", if, indeed, there is one.'

The Foreign Office helped Philby to obtain posts as Middle East correspondent with the *Observer* and the *Economist* in 1956. He lived there until 1962 when, with a CIA hit-man on his tail and British intelligence trying to recall him to London (probably as a prelude to arrest) he disappeared. It was not until 1963 that Philby's role as 'the Third Man' became public. By this time he too was safely installed in Russia, with Soviet citizenship and the rank of honorary colonel in the KGB. The full story only came out in a series of *Sunday Times* articles in October 1967 and Philby died, an avowed Communist, in 1988.

ANTHONY BLUNT

Blunt's activities as a spy became known to the authorities when he confessed in 1964, in the wake of Philby's disappearance and in the light of evidence supplied by the Americans. He made his confession in return for immunity from prosecution and it was only in 1979 that the government admitted his role publicly, after Labour Member of Parliament Ted Leadbetter directly challenged Margaret Thatcher about the matter.

Blunt was another of the Cambridge Apostles. He spied for Russia from the 1930s onwards, making it a racing certainty that he would be offered a position in British intelligence. Sure enough, he was recruited by MI5 in 1940. His war record included giving details of the Normandy landings to the Russians (from whom their allies were very keen to keep it secret) and sending many thousands of Soviet exiles back to what can most optimistically be described as an uncertain future in Russia. Blunt made considerable use of his homosexuality to blackmail potential informants and also assisted in the defection of Burgess and Maclean in 1951. Fortunately for him, he was one of those brought in to search Burgess's flat after his defection, giving him the opportunity to pocket some highly incriminating material about himself and Philby. Blunt was first investigated as a possible spy at this time, but made a successful denial.

Meanwhile, he had become a considerable Establishment figure. A distinguished art historian, he was made Surveyor of the Royal Art Collection in 1945 (a position he held until 1972, many years after his record of spying was known to the authorities) and Director of the Courtauld Institute of Art (1947–74). He was knighted in 1956 for his services to art, a title that was annulled in 1979. It was then that the book *Climate of Treason* was published, fictionalising Blunt as a character called Maurice. This disguise was soon blown by *Private Eye*, leading to Margaret Thatcher reading out to Parliament the statement which had been on Blunt's file for many years, in anticipation of just such an eventuality.

AND TWO OF OURS –
GREVILLE WYNNE AND JAMES BOND

In December 1960 a delegation of British machine tool manufacturers went to Moscow in search of business. Their leader was a businessman named Greville Wynne. While there, Wynne was approached by a senior figure from Soviet military intelligence, Colonel Oleg Penkovsky, who had been assigned to act as minder to Wynne, but instead asked for a message to be passed to the CIA about his wish to defect. Wynne had been recruited by MI5 as long ago as 1939, and later by MI6. He acted as a go-between on his next visit to Russia, returning with a package of secret documents and news that Penkovsky was coming to Britain with a delegation within a few days. Penkovsky was duly won over and Wynne acted as his contact during his visits to Moscow. Eventually Wynne's repeated visits, with little apparent sign of business activity to justify them, began to attract the attention of the Soviet authorities. Problems also emerged in relation to Wynne's inability to keep silent, sober or celibate during his visits.

In August 1962 Penkovsky was arrested. In his confession he revealed the connection with Wynne. The following November a trap was set for Wynne in Budapest. He was arrested and flown to Moscow, just as Russia was being made to suffer the humiliation of dismantling its Cuban missile sites. Wynne maintained that he was an innocent businessman until he discovered that Penkovsky was also in custody, at which point he started to confess. While the Foreign Office stoutly denied Wynne's connection with them to the House of Commons, the Russians staged a public trial. Wynne got eight years' imprisonment and Penkovsky was executed in May 1963.

Wynne was 'swapped' for Gordon Lonsdale in April 1964 and returned to England. In public, he initially maintained his position as an innocent businessman who had been tortured by the KGB. In private, he wrangled with the SIS over the compensation he demanded for the destruction of his business. Eventually he saw a better chance of reimbursement by admitting his involvement – or, rather, a highly coloured and fictionalised version of it – which he published with great commercial success as *The Man from Moscow*. The government, having denied it all, was suitably embarrassed.

But by the 1960s we all knew what a life of espionage was really like, courtesy of Mr Ian Fleming's creation. James Bond was said to have been an amalgam of Fleming himself (he had been in Naval Intelligence, and shared Bond's partiality for dry martinis and caviar) and two others, one of whom was Sidney Reilly, a British spy who disappeared in Russia in the 1920s. The name James Bond was taken from the author of one of Fleming's favourite books, *Birds of the West Indies* (before anyone says a word, it was about ornithology).

Bond's original – and some say best – screen persona was the Edinburgh-born former milkman, lifeguard, bodybuilder, artist's model and coffin-polisher, Sean Connery. The first Bond film, *Doctor No*, was launched, with immaculate timing, just as the Cuban missile crisis was breaking and it was one of the smash hits of the year. Connery went on to

James Bond spawned a host of imitations and a wealth of merchandising.

play Bond in several more films, allegedly being paid £3.5 million for his appearance in *Never Say Never Again* in 1983. Not every reviewer of *Doctor No* was an instant convert:

> There is . . . about him a faint Irish-American look and sound, which somehow spoils the image. . . . Perhaps Mr Sean Connery will, with more practice, get the 'feel' of the part a little more surely than he does here.
>
> For the rest, Dr No is a carefully, expertly made . . . exercise in violence and sadism so shaped that the audience is conditioned into believing that it is witnessing the last word in sophisticated thrills, decked out with even more sophisticated trimmings of sex.

Fleming died of a heart attack while playing golf in August 1964, just as his creation was beginning to make him seriously rich and famous.

Economic crisis is good news for some – the government was forced to devalue the pound by 14 per cent in 1967.

CHRONICLE OF THE 1960S: HIGH FINANCE

1960: Average weekly wage £14 10s 8d.

10 September 1963: American Express card launched in Britain, but only for those with an annual income of over £2,000.

21 February 1964: First £10 notes issued.

24 May 1965: Decision to move to a decimal currency announced.

1 February 1966: The first £25,000 Premium Bond winner.

29 June 1966: Barclaycard – Britain's first widely available credit card – is introduced.

27 June 1967: World's first cash dispenser is introduced, at Barclays Bank, Enfield.

23 April 1968: First decimal coins introduced.

13 September 1968: Banks open on a Saturday for the last time.

14 October 1969: The 50 pence coin is introduced.

1969: Average weekly wage – £24 16s 5d.

These pupils learned the mysteries of metrication through song.

A decimal supermarket, set up to help people understand the new money.

1968 – banks announce their last Saturday opening.

Decimalisation began to be introduced in 1968, to bewilder the public and encourage sales of early computers.

BANKING HOURS OF BUSINESS

On and after **1st July, 1969,** Clearing Bank Branches will be closed on Saturdays and will be open for business on

Monday to Friday
9.30 a.m. to 3.30 p.m.

except for the Town Clearing Branches in the City of London, which will be open from 9.30 a.m. to 3.00 p.m.

In addition, most Branches will be open from

4.30 p.m. to 6.00 p.m.

on **one evening in the week** (but not Friday).

All transactions undertaken during this late session will be recorded in the books of the Banks under the date of the following business day.

Notices will be displayed by Branches showing the day of the week on which they will be open from 4.30 p.m.

**BARCLAYS BANK · COUTTS & CO · DISTRICT BANK
GLYN MILLS & CO · LLOYDS BANK
MARTINS BANK · MIDLAND BANK · NATIONAL BANK
NATIONAL PROVINCIAL BANK
WESTMINSTER BANK · WILLIAMS DEACON'S BANK**

CHAPTER 4

ALL YOU NEED IS LOVE – AND A GOOD AGENT: 1960s POP

Out of pop there has now grown a substantial movement of . . .
performers who aim to express themselves with some seriousness of
purpose.

David Hughes in *Discrimination and Popular Culture*
(ed. Denys Thompson)

Wild thing, you make my heart sing,
You make everything groovy, wild thing.

The Troggs – who were not part of that movement

Pop music began the 1960s in poor shape. Many of the artists who had injected the excitement into 1950s rock and roll were out of contention for one reason or another. For Elvis, it was due to military service; for Buddy Holly, a bad choice of airline; Little Richard had found God and Jerry Lee Lewis had made what we can most kindly describe as 'an unsuitable marriage'. Payola scandals had hit the American industry and there were signs of a concerted attack on rock and roll. The television authorities in Britain set up a joint committee which castigated pop music for lyrics that were 'degraded and injurious; . . . too many of the lyrics broadcast are merely drivel and have a generally debasing tone which is to be deprecated.' In the USA, *Variety* magazine launched its own attack in March 1960:

Rock and Roll's global wane: strong trend to standards
The de-emphasis of the rock and roll beat, which has been marked in the United States since the start of payola problems a few months ago, is being echoed in Europe as well. . . . Among the Europeans themselves . . . the big beat never really established a firm hold on the

market, except for a few stand-up artists like Elvis Presley and Bill Haley. Now the traditional European emphasis on melodic material is reasserting itself.

Elvis came back from military service singing ballads, rather than rocking. He did not even feature in the 1960 *Billboard* top ten male singers, which was won by Frank Sinatra. Our own Elvis substitute, Cliff Richard, had also gone mainstream, making films and publishing his autobiography after a career which had then spanned a full two years. The payola scandal in America harmed the independent small companies, which had often produced the more adventurous records. Unable to compete with the publicity budgets and distribution networks of the big companies, they used to bribe disc jockeys to play their records as a way of evening things up. When this was stopped, the bigger companies, with their more conservative lists, had a far greater hold over the industry.

It was from this unpromising start that the swinging 1960s were born. One of the major influences spent the early part of the decade learning the trade in Germany. Their first record, *My Bonnie*, was released under the name of Tony Sheridan and the Beat Brothers, since their record company, Polydor, thought that German customers would confuse their name – the Beatles – with 'peedles', the German slang word for the tummy banana.

Why did the early 1960s spawn such a wealth of British groups? Some leading lights of the period – such as Dave Clark and Ringo Starr – put it down to the ending of conscription. This, they argued, left many young people lacking any direction and looking for an escape from their sometimes dreary everyday existence. Another important influence was skiffle, which had created an interest in blues-based participatory music in the 1950s. The Beatles actually started out as a skiffle group. Skiffle itself emerged more or less by accident. A trumpeter in a trad jazz band, Ken Colyer, suffered from a weak lip that needed to be rested during a set. In order to give him a break, a number of the band members formed their own little combo, to play a sub-set of blues numbers. These soon became

ALWAYS NUMBER 1 FOR POP RECORDS

W H S

W. H. SMITH & SON

16, NORTH STREET, CHICHESTER
Telephone 82013

more popular than the rest of the band's act and their guitarist, Lonnie Donegan, set up on his own. The name skiffle was derived from a term used by New Orleans negroes for their parties, at which they used to play music to raise the money for their rent. Another way in which the influence of blues made itself felt was through the great Cunard liners that plied between Liverpool and the United States (helping to explain the importance of that city in the pop revolution of the 1960s). The staff working on the ships heard the blues on their visits to the States and brought records back home with them, to play to their friends.

THE OTHER STARS OF THE 1960S

The lives and careers of stars such as the Beatles and the Rolling Stones are too well known to require further detailed repetition here (with some exceptions, as we shall see). Instead, let's look at some of the lesser lights of the 1960s, who made their more esoteric but none the less distinctive contributions to the popular music of the decade.

Tiny Tim

He sang in a strangled falsetto that suggested excessively tight underwear

Born Herbert Buckingham Khaury so long ago that he was almost a contemporary of Charles Dickens (from whose character he took his stage name), Tiny Tim was one of the oddest pop phenomena of the decade. He was gangling and snaggle-toothed, with long straggly hair, and he sang in a strangled falsetto that suggested excessively tight underwear. He accompanied himself on the ukelele, an instrument most people thought had been deservedly consigned to history with the passing of George Formby.

Tim – who had also appeared under the stage names Darry Dover, Larry Love, Emmett Swink, Texicali Tex and Judas Foxglove – was an only child who grew up surrounded by music hall songs and popular pre-war crooners like Al Bowlly and Rudy Vallee. Early work experience at the MGM studios persuaded him that his future was as a singing star, however strongly his appearance suggested otherwise. He began playing in small clubs in New York.

He gradually became better known, and he performed in the film *You Are What You Eat*, which also featured rock stars Paul Butterfield, Electric Flag and Barry McGuire. He appeared on the Johnny Carson television show and became a regular on *Rowan and Martin's Laugh-in* – the 1960s comedy programme which proved that form could triumph over content. He is particularly remembered – not necessarily fondly – for his revival of the 1929 song *Tiptoe through the Tulips*. This went into the top twenty in the States and the accompanying album sold 150,000 copies in four months. It was not a hit in Britain, though football fans adapted his song for their own, less delicate, purposes:

'Tiptoe down the South End,
With your boots on
Get your heads kicked in . . .'

Tim had slightly greater success in Britain with his improbable rendition of Jerry Lee Lewis's *Great Balls of Fire*, which reached number 45 in 1969.

At the end of the 1960s, Tim's star shone very brightly indeed. He recorded with The Band, headed a sell-out concert at the Royal Albert Hall and appeared on the Beatles' 1968 fan club Christmas disc, singing his version of the Lennon and McCartney song *Nowhere Man*. So camp-looking that he made Kenneth Williams seem like a candidate to play James Bond, Tim belied those who had their doubts about him by marrying a girl young enough to be his daughter. The wedding to seventeen-year-old Miss Vicki (Victoria May Budinger) took place live on the Johnny Carson Show in 1969 in front of an audience estimated at forty million. Although as a devout Christian he held some unfashionably firm views about chastity, he overcame them sufficiently to produce a daughter, predictably named Tulip, before the marriage broke up in 1972. Miss Vicky went off, supporting herself by becoming a go-go dancer. She spurned Tim's romantic offer to take her back if she passed a test for venereal disease, divorce following in 1977. Tim got custody of the ukelele.

Tim's fame was short-lived. His career was not helped by the release of an early recording, made in 1962, which Tim himself described as 'the worst-ever recorded album in the history of music'. Some 100,000 customers bought it, thinking it was the official second album – and were disappointed. Those who saw him merely as a comic freak-show missed the fact that Tim was a gifted, if eccentric, interpreter of the music he grew up with. His first album attracted some high praise from some very respectable quarters. Albert Goldman said in the *New York Times*:

Popular chanteuse Miss Marianne Faithfull . . . and her one-time consort Mr Mick Jagger of the Rolling Stones.

The album is a dream theatre that echoes beguilingly with all the voices of Tiny Tim. To say that these are the most perfect impersonations of old singers ever heard would hardly do justice to the art that has re-embodied these entertainers in electronic avatars, summoning them up out of the past to caper again before a strobe-lit oleo.

Life magazine spoke no less highly of it: 'One of the most dazzling albums of programmed entertainment to come along since the Beatles introduced that new genre into pop with *Sgt Pepper's Lonely Hearts Club Band*. If *Sgt Pepper* was a wide-screen epic, Tiny's album is a full-length feature animated cartoon, with Tiny doing all the voices.'

After the initial flush of success, Tim continued to record. He supplemented his musical career with appearances on chat shows, the B-movie 'slasher' film *Blood Harvest* and even a cameo appearance on the television show *Roseanne*. There were signs of a revival of interest in him in the 1990s, but his health was already in decline. He died as he would have wished, in November 1996, suffering a fatal heart attack just as he came off stage at a charity concert.

Screaming Lord Sutch – an adornment to both the musical and the political spheres in the 1960s.

Screaming Lord Sutch

Until such time as someone spots that Alec Douglas-Home was a member of the Supremes, 'Lord' David Sutch remains the only pop star ever to go on to lead a political party. He was one of the first stars to sport long hair (as long ago as 1960) and his band, the Savages, proved a training ground for a number of musicians who went on to greater things, such as Richie Blackmore, Nicky Hopkins and Paul Nicholas. Even bigger names – Jimmy Page, Jeff Beck, Keith Moon, Noel Redding and John Bonham – also recorded with him, and his records were produced by the legendary Joe Meek. He was inspired by the rock legend Screaming Jay Hawkins, who began his act from inside a coffin and who carried around with him a flaming (in the incendiary, rather than the expletive, sense) skull named Henry. But it was Sutch who added the finesse of a necklace made from a toilet seat. His repertoire included such gems as *Jack the Ripper*,

Monster in Black Tights (a spoof of *Venus in Blue Jeans*), *All Black and Hairy*, *Screem and Screem*, *She's fallen in love with the Monster Man*, *Dracula's Daughter* and *Murder in the Graveyard*. He was definitely one of the new romantics.

Seeking wider fame, he diversified into pirate radio, and began broadcasting Radio Sutch from an old fort on the Shivering Sands off Whitstable in May 1964. It was hopelessly under-capitalised, and Sutch found himself exchanging free advertising for essential daily supplies. He sold out later that year to entrepreneur Reg Calvert, who changed the station's name to Radio City (also known as The Tower of Power, from its 200ft mast). Calvert was later shot dead in a dispute over the ownership of the station, in true pirate tradition.

Despite his promising pedigree, Sutch was never to grace the top thirty. He went on to achieve greater fame as a politician. He began by standing for the National Teenage Party – this at a time when the minimum voting age was twenty-one. He then turned from one disenfranchised group to another – the insane – becoming the leader of the Monster Raving Loony Party. He led the party from 1983 to his death in 1999, exposing the inconsistency of the mainstream parties' leadership. Under his control, they belied their name by offering a beacon of sanity in the mad world of politics. Their policies included having all chartered accountants set in concrete and used as traffic islands; making wigs not only available on the NHS but also compulsory; reducing the length of the unemployment queues by making people stand closer together; calling for there to be more than one Monopolies Commission; and towing the British Isles 500 miles south into the Atlantic, to improve the climate. Their time must surely come.

Their policies included having all chartered accountants set in concrete and used as traffic islands

Serge Gainsbourg

Frenchman Serge Gainsbourg was another unlikely pop idol, with a face that looked like an unmade bed, suggesting that he had seen a lot of life. Born Lucien Ginzburg in Paris in 1928, the son of an exiled Russian Jew, he was thought of more as an actor (specialising in villains and creeps), artist, film-writer, screenwriter, film director and a composer of material for others than a pop star in his own right – until he came up with *Je t'aime . . . moi non plus* in 1969. This song was breathed, rather than sung, over a sleazy organ track and the simulated sounds of sexual congress (at least, one assumes they were simulated). It was originally written for Brigitte Bardot but, as we now know, the only animal noises of interest to her were those made by real animals. Gainsbourg had previously also worked with Petula Clark and Nana Mouskouri, but they were perhaps not quite the image he had in mind. The piece was therefore recorded by him with his third wife Jane Birkin, a British woman subsequently adopted by the French as a sex symbol, with a taste in fashion that made page three girls look overdressed. It will come as no surprise to learn that they were voted France's most exciting couple of 1969.

The BBC banned the record, so it was naturally a huge success – so much so that the controversy surrounding it scared the original producers,

Philips, into selling the recording on to another smaller company, Major Minor Records, just as it reached number two in the charts. It went on to be a number one hit all over Europe and also made the hot hundred in America. After the BBC ban, a group called Sounds Nice released an instrumental version of the piece, under the title *Love at First Sight*, and *Private Eye* produced a splendid spoof version of it on their 1969 free Christmas record. There was even a version produced by Frankie Howerd and June Whitfield, called *Up Je t'aime* (we can safely assume that the 'Up' in this case does not refer to up-market). In Britain it was the second best selling single of 1969, beaten only by Frank Sinatra and *My Way*.

The record enjoyed further success when revived in 1974 but the immediate follow-up – *69 Année Erotique* – bombed. Perhaps less surprising was the failure of the dance craze that Gainsbourg tried to launch – *La Decadanse* – which involved the male gyrating with his groin pressed against his partner's bottom and his hands over her breasts (though it would certainly have given a new dimension to *Come Dancing*).

During the 1970s, Gainsbourg's various productions each tried to outdo the last in outrageousness (with the possible exception of his second-placed entry for the 1990 Eurovision Song Contest). He suffered his first heart attack in 1973 and his last on 3 March 1991, and is remembered variously as a 'misunderstood genius' and a 'cynical old lecher'.

> *He is remembered variously as a 'misunderstood genius' and a 'cynical old lecher'*

BONZOS, BOWLERS, TWISTERS AND TROGLODYTES: A STROLL THROUGH 1960s POP

The Bonzo Dog Doodah Band was formed by art students and was originally known as the Bonzo Dog Dada Band. However, this reference to the artistic movement that anticipated surrealism was lost on most of their audience, who simply thought they were a 1920s revival group. So Doodah it became (a case of dada-ing Dada, if I am not mistaken). Their initial performances were informal in the extreme (to the extent that they were never quite sure who was going to turn up to play) but they were to set the scene for future parodists of the pop industry, such as The Rutles (in which leading Bonzo Neil Innes teamed up with Monty Python's Eric Idle) and Spinal Tap. The entire band appeared on television with parts of the Monty Python team in the show *Do Not Adjust Your Set* and they also became associated with the Beatles. Paul McCartney produced their best-known hit *I'm the Urban Spaceman* under the pseudonym Apollo C. Vermouth in 1968, and they appeared in the Beatles' bewildering film *Magical Mystery Tour*, performing their *Death Cab for Cutie*.

The Bonzos satirised many musical forms – *Jazz: delicious hot, disgusting cold, Can blue men sing the whites?* – and the pretensions of rock opera with *Keynsham*, their spoof of the genre, which was based on singer Viv Stanshall's experiences in a mental hospital. *My pink half of the drainpipe* was a hymn to suburbia and *The intro and the outro* was simply weird. Their records were worth purchasing for the song titles alone – who could resist *Humanoid Boogie*, *We are normal* and *The Doughnut in Granny's Greenhouse*?

The changing sartorial standards of the 1960s. The Shadows (top) from early in the decade, and the less formal attire of Pink Floyd from the late 1960s.

Bernard Stanley Bilk may well be the only claim to fame of Pensford, Somerset, where he was born in 1929, the son of a Methodist preacher. His big break came about as the unlikely result of falling asleep while doing guard duty in the army in Egypt in 1947. During the subsequent three-month prison sentence he started to learn the clarinet. By 1954 he was good enough to win a place in the Ken Colyer Jazz Band, and he went

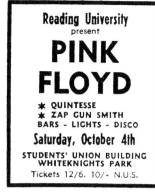

Reading University
present
PINK
FLOYD
★ QUINTESSE
★ ZAP GUN SMITH
BARS - LIGHTS - DISCO
Saturday, October 4th
STUDENTS' UNION BUILDING
WHITEKNIGHTS PARK
Tickets 12/6. 10/- N.U.S.

on to form his own Paramount Jazz Band in 1955, which he led under the title of Mr Acker Bilk (Acker being a Somerset term for 'friend'). They had a couple of minor hits in 1960 and 1961, and then Bilk wrote an instrumental piece which he called Jenny after one of his daughters. It was taken up as the theme tune of a children's television programme and renamed after the programme.

Few people will now remember a television programme called *Stranger on the Shore* but its theme tune spent fifty-five weeks in the British pop charts (without ever becoming number one). It also spent twenty-one weeks in the American charts, where it did reach the top, and sold a total of four million copies in five years. Bilk was invited to play at the 1961 Royal Variety Performance on the back of its success. Bilk bucked the sartorial conventions of 1960s pop stardom, and is quite possibly the only man to top the American charts wearing a bowler hat and striped waistcoat (though, if he is not, I do *not* wish to know about it). He enjoyed further chart success in 1976 and, when last heard of, was still touring and dining out on the strength of his greatest hit.

Chubby Checker was born Ernest Evans in Philadelphia in 1941. He spent the first part of his working life removing feathers from poultry (points will be deducted from anybody making jokes about pheasant pluckers). His first

Mr Acker Bilk, for once without his bowler hat.

wife told him that he looked rather like a smaller version of Fats Domino, and it was from this that he derived his stage name. In 1958 a group called Hank Ballard and the Midnighters released a record called *The Twist*. In its original form it was an earthy R&B number, but it was not until Checker's 1960 version came out that the song – and the dance craze – really took off. The record sold three million copies and spawned a positive barrage of merchandising. There were twist clothes, twist shoes, twist pyjamas, twist sweets, twist hats and even twist hairstyles that gyrated in time with their proud owners (though, to get the full benefit, you would have to take off your twist hat first). Really sad individuals attempted to screw themselves into the ground for days at a time in order to enter the *Guinness Book of Records* for the dance. Hollywood even brought out films such as *Hey, Let's Twist* and

This couple came second in their twist competition. No doubt the absence of twist hats told against them.

Don't Knock the Twist, none of which starred Sir Laurence Olivier.

In Britain it took longer to get going, and it was the sequel, memorably entitled *Let's Twist Again*, that climbed to number two in the British charts and spent thirty-four weeks there. Records came complete with instructions on how to perform the dance. You were asked to imagine stubbing out a cigarette with both feet at the same time, while simultaneously drying your back with a towel, though why you should be attempting both activities at once is a question that was perhaps mercifully left unanswered. One distinct disadvantage to the twist, compared, say, with the waltz, was the health risk. In one week in October 1961, the New York Safety Council reported that 49 out of the 54 cases of back injury reported to them were the result of over-enthusiastic twisting. One man, twisting at a dance organised by his office, suffered a heart attack and died. However, since this took place in America, the widow was able to sue the socks (twisting socks, no doubt) off her late husband's employer.

By 1962 Checker's fame was such that he married a former Miss World, Catherina Lodders of Holland. The craze he had started attracted a host of imitators, including records such as *Twist and Shout* (the Isley Brothers and the Beatles), *Twisting the Night Away* (Sam Cooke) and *The Twisting Postman* (artiste happily unknown). When the public tired of twisting, Checker tried other dance crazes. He enjoyed some success with *The Fly* and *Limbo Rock*, but *The Jet*, *The Swim* and *The Freddie* sank without trace. I leave it to future generations of anthropologists, or possibly physiotherapists, to hunt down the instructions for them.

The Troggs began as the Troglodytes in 1964, a four-piece band performing around the Andover area of Hampshire. Early changes in personnel forced guitarist Reginald Ball to take over as the reluctant lead vocalist. They performed material by the Kinks, and it was when the Kinks' manager Larry Page saw them and decided to work with them that their career took off. They shortened their name to the Troggs and recorded the debut single *Lost Girl*, written by Ball. It got lost more comprehensively than the girl in the title.

Two months later Page received the sheet music for two more songs. One was *Did you ever have to make up your mind?* by John Sebastian of the Loving Spoonful – which was not obvious troglodyte material. The other was a Chip Taylor composition which, unpromisingly, had bombed when recorded by an American band, the Wild Ones. Page had some trouble persuading the Troggs to record the rubbishy lyrics of *Wild Thing*, but from a commercial point of view it was probably the best day's work he ever did.

It went to number two in the British charts in May 1966 and topped the American Hundred for two weeks, selling over a million records. It was at this point that Reginald Ball became Reg Presley, naming himself after his idol, Elvis (that's not Costello – his first names were, of course, Abbott And). A series of further grunt and groan hits followed, including *With a Girl Like You*, *I can't control myself*, *Give it to me* and *Any way that you Want Me*. At this point, the group's fortunes went into a decline. Their problems led to an acrimonious court case against their former manager and the disbanding of the group in 1969.

An American cult following, apparently fuelled by a bootlegged tape of one of their recording sessions including some picturesque Hampshire filthy language, led to the re-forming of the group in 1972. Cover versions of (*I can't get no*) *Satisfaction* and *Good Vibrations* died the death, but the use of the *Wild Thing* theme in advertisements and the television programme *Gladiators* kept them in the public eye. Presley the composer hit the jackpot in 1995, when his song *Love is all around* was recorded by the group Wet Wet Wet for the film *Four Weddings and a Funeral*, earning him over £1 million in royalties.

No review of 1960s pop could end without mention of the man who bestrode the decade's charts like a colossus. He started the 1960s with a worldwide top ten hit, and his popularity was undimmed by the time of his 1962 success, in which he introduced British audiences to world music,

Remember them?

years before Paul Simon and others jumped on the bandwagon. The decade closed with him taking a song that had been written sixty years before and turning it into Britain's best-selling single of 1969. As recently as 1993 he proved his versatility and staying power by taking a song by one of our leading heavy metal bands into the top ten. I refer of course to Mr Rolf Harris, and his songs *Tie me Kangaroo down, Sport*; *Sun arise*; *Two Little Boys* and *Stairway to Heaven*.

PIRACY ON THE HIGH SEAS

Britain's listening habits, and the whole way in which popular music was presented, were transformed in the 1960s by a group of illegal broadcasters operating outside the nation's territorial waters. Evidence that there was a demand for something a little more modern than the BBC's Light Programme (something at least set in the twentieth century would have been nice) had been established as long ago as 1933 by Radio Luxembourg. In 1960 the ship *Veronica* moored off the Dutch coast and its broadcasts to mainland Europe were also picked up in Britain. When the BBC refused to play a record by Georgie Fame, the man responsible for its promotion – a 27-year-old self-styled Roman Catholic anarchist named Rohan O'Rahilly – took it to *Veronica*. Seeing the potential of the station, O'Rahilly bought a 1930 vintage passenger ferry called *Frederica*. With a quick change of name to *Caroline*, in honour of President Kennedy's daughter, he moored the boat off Felixstowe. On 29 March 1964 Simon Dee uttered the words 'Good morning, ladies and gentlemen. This is Radio Caroline, broadcasting on 199, your all-day music station' – and the golden age of radio piracy had begun. Soon a rival moored nearby – the ship formerly known as *Mi Amigo*, renamed *Radio Atlanta*. A merger soon followed and the original *Caroline* sailed off to moor near the Isle of Man, leaving *Mi Amigo* to continue broadcasting as Caroline (South).

The pirate stations were a huge success, attracting millions away from the turgid offerings of the old stations. A survey in September 1964 showed that Radio Caroline was getting more listeners than the BBC. Many others followed in their wake, broadcasting from locations as varied as an ex-US Navy minesweeper and disused marine forts to a trawler which had once been the pride of the Ross fish-finger fleet. But the pirate stations were not limited to those broadcasting top twenty hits. Radio 390 was operated by novelist Ted Albeury from a fort in the Thames estuary. Its well-groomed and respectable presenters brought their listeners such cutting edge programmes as *Masters of the Organ* and *Tea Time Tunes*. But being polite cut no ice with the Ministry. They discovered a sandbank just beyond the fort, which moved it

Remember him?

EDDIE FRIDAY says:
A D.J. of great renown
Tony
Blackburn
is coming to town
IN PERSON HE'LL BE
THERE FOR ALL TO SEE
DON'T FORGET THE DATE—Write it down
FRIDAY, OCTOBER 31

The people who played the records became almost as famous as those who made them. Pirate DJ Simon Dee opens a young and trendy supermarket . . . while Alan Freeman attracts a rather more mature audience to his opening.

from international waters to home waters – and therefore within their jurisdiction, and they promptly closed it down. There were even some distinctly land-based stations. Radio Fiona was operated from 1969 by two brothers in Hertfordshire, a county not noted for its dramatic coastal scenery, except at the very highest of tides.

The pirate operations very quickly attracted the wrath of the authorities. For one thing, it was said that they interfered with the radio frequencies used for ship-to-shore communications and the lifeguard service. For another, Phonographic Performance Limited was after them for non-payment of royalties to the artists they broadcast and which PPL represented. They were also politically incorrect. The Postmaster General, Mr Short, said that he did not deplore the entertainment content of the radio programmes, but was unhappy about their political and propaganda-type broadcasts, all of which had so far been anti-Labour. Surely, he asked, the opposition realised the terrible potential of this kind of development? The answer was probably that the opposition was secretly gleeful about their attacks.

The pirates were extreme examples of capitalist-free enterprise, and thus represented everything an unreformed Labour government detested. They tried to get the International Telecommunications Union to close the stations down, and the Postmaster General announced in the Commons that they were investigating the possibility of jamming them. It even turned out to be an offence under the Wireless Telegraphy Act 1949 for a member of the public to listen to a pirate radio broadcast, though quite how they would have enforced such a law takes some imagining. There were nine pirate stations broadcasting by the time the authorities finally got the Marine Broadcasting (Offences) Act passed in 1967. This made it illegal to advertise through the stations or to supply the pirates with any goods or services from the mainland. Most of the stations decided to close down at this point, but *Caroline* fought on, getting all necessary supplies from Holland and continuing to broadcast sporadically until the 1980s.

The ban came into effect from August 1967. In the preceding month the BBC announced its own response to pirate broadcasting. In a major shake-up of the networks, Radios 1, 2, 3 and 4 were established, with Radio 1 being seen as the direct replacement for pirate radio. It was to start broadcasting from 30 September and Robin Scott, Controller of Light Programmes, acknowledged the BBC's debt to the pirates:

> We have a professional admiration for what they have done. It would be foolish to pretend we are not using some of the techniques of the commercial stations. Jingles, slogans and internal publicity for the station will be going out between records, and that sort of thing. But we will want to avoid the mid-Atlantic style they have created. I am sure there are good British disc-jockeys who will create their own style.

He even went on to promise 'live, warm-hearted, swinging programmes', the little raver. And how did they create this distinctively un-piratical approach to popular broadcasting? Why, by recruiting all the pirate disc jockeys, of course! When Radio 1's line-up was announced in September, it included Tony Blackburn, Kenny Everett, Emperor Rosco, Ed Stewart, John Peel and Mike Raven, to name just some of the better known of the reformed pirate presenters. The only difference was that instead of saying 'Caroline on 199, your all-day music station', they were now handing out badges saying 'I'm a Radio 1-up man' and 'Ring-a-247-Ding'.

Now, there's progress for you.

CHRONICLE OF THE 1960s: EUROVISION

Ever since 1956 the Eurovision Song Contest has provided the pinnacle of the cultural year for millions of music lovers. Of course, nobody watches it for the banal jingles submitted by all those foreigners, most of them in languages that civilised people cannot even understand. It is the epic quality of the British entries that alone makes it a feast for the ears. It is thus particularly galling that it took us until 1967 to win it. Here, for posterity, is a full list of those unjustly overlooked masterpieces of the 1960s:

1960 Looking High, High, High – Bryan Johnson
1961 Are you sure? – The Allisons
1962 Ring a Ding Girl – Ronnie Carroll
1963 Say wonderful things – Ronnie Carroll
1964 I love the Little Things – Matt Monro
1965 I belong – Kathy Kirby
1966 A Man Without Love – Kenneth McKellar
1967 Puppet on a String – Sandie Shaw
1968 Congratulations – Cliff Richard
1969 Boom Bang a Bang – Lulu

*Sir Harold Webb and Ronald Wycherley sign somebody
else's names in their fans' autograph books . . . while
Dave Clark sticks with his own.*

Elvis Who?

Mr Presley was indeed christened Elvis, but not everybody's parents had the foresight to give their offspring suitable names for their future rock and roll careers. Here is a guide to the true identities of a range of 1960s pop stars:

Marc Bolan – Mark Feld
Sonny Bono – Salvatore Phillip Bono
Captain Beefheart – Don van Vliet
Freddy Cannon – Freddy Picariello
Cher – Cherilyn Sarkasian LaPier
Eric Clapton – Eric Patrick Clapp
Lou Christie – Lugee Alfredo Giovanni Sacco
Bobby Darin – Walden Robert Casotto
Bo Diddley – Elias Bates
Bob Dylan – Robert Allen Zimmerman
Fabian – Fabiano Forte Bonaparte
Adam Faith – Terence Nelhams
Georgie Fame – Clive Powell
Wayne Fontana – Glyn Ellis
Emile Ford – Emile Sweetman
Connie Francis – Concetta Rosa Maria Franconero
Billy Fury – Ronald Wycherley
Englebert Humperdinck – Arnold George Dorsey
Mick Jagger – Michael Philip
Brian Jones – Lewis Brian Hopkin-Jones
Eden Kane – Richard Sarstedt
Billy J. Kramer – William Howard Ashton
Manfred Mann – Manfred Liebowitz
Hank Marvin – Brian Rankin
Matt Munro – Terry Parsons
P.J. Proby – James Marcus Smith
Cliff Richard – Harry Roger Webb
Del Shannon – Charles Westover
Sandy Shaw – Sandra Goodrich
Dusty Springfield – Mary O'Brien
Cat Stevens – Steven Georgiou
Tina Turner – Anna Mae Bullock
Twinkle – Lynne Annette Ripley
Ricky Valence – David Spencer
Frankie Vaughan – Frank Abelson
Stevie Wonder – Steveland Judkins
Bill Wyman – William Perks
Mark Wynter – Terence Lewis

But nobody went to as much trouble to change their name as Walter Carlos, who became Wendy Carlos – with the assistance of a little surgery. I've always wondered – are the patients allowed to keep the bits left over?

Terence Nelhams, incognito at the Manchester Hippodrome.

IT'S TOP OF THE POPS

How far did the pop revolution of the 1960s transform the top ten? Not as much as you'd think, to judge from these charts from the opposite ends of the decade. Was all Mick Jagger's pouting and hip swivelling in vain?

January 1960

1. What do you want to make those eyes at me for? – Emile Ford
2. What do you want? – Adam Faith
3. Oh! Carol – Neil Sedaka
4. Seven little girls sitting in the back seat – the Avons
5. Johnny Staccato theme – Elmer Bernstein
6. Little White Bull – Tommy Steele
7. Bad Boy – Marty Wilde
8. Reveille Rock – Johnny and the Hurricanes
9. Travellin' light – Cliff Richard
10. Some kind'a Earthquake – Duane Eddy

December 1969

1. Sugar sugar – the Archies
2. Yester-me, yester-you, yesterday – Stevie Wonder
3. Ruby, don't take your love to town – Kenny Rogers and the First Edition
4. (Call me) Number One – The Tremoloes
5. Two Little Boys – Rolf Harris
6. Oh Well – Fleetwood Mac
7. Melting Pot – Blue Mink
8. Something/Come Together – The Beatles
9. Sweet Dream – Jethro Tull
10. Suspicious Minds – Elvis Presley

SHE LOVES YOU? NAH, NAH, NAH!

Those who lived through the 1960s will know the history of the Beatles' triumphs more or less by heart. Just for a change, let's follow the Beatles through all the low points of their career in the 1960s:

5 May 1960: The Beetals (as they then spelt it) fail an audition to be Billy Fury's backing band.

July 1960: The Silver Beatles (as they have now become) play a gig in Liverpool – backing a stripper named Janice. They may not have been the focus of attention.

July 1960: a very short-lived Beatle, drummer Norman Chapman, joins the band on 9 July and leaves it on 23 July. (Just as well, really – John, Paul, George and . . . Norman? I don't think so).

4 October 1960: They are banned from the Indra Club, Hamburg, for playing too loud.

21 November 1960: George Harrison is deported from Germany for being under age.

29 November 1960: Paul McCartney and Pete Best (the then drummer) are jailed for arson, then deported.

SUN. APRIL 10 FOR 7 DAYS. Sun. from 5. Daily Cont. from 1-25.
L.C.P. 8-40.

GRAND HOLIDAY ALL (U) PROGRAMME IN COLOUR

The BEATLES

in

HELP !

(U).

Sun. 5, 8-35. Daily 1-25, 5, 8-50

Frank Sinatra, Dean Martin, Sammy Davis Jnr.

SERGEANTS THREE

(U).

Sun. 6-30. Daily 2-55, 6-40.

The Beatles were frequently in need of help in the 1960s.

17 December 1960: Another short-lived Beatle, bassist Chas Newby, joins 17 December and leaves 31 December.

1 January 1962: The Beatles audition for a recording contract with Decca – and are turned down.

10 April 1962: Former Beatle Stuart Sutcliffe dies.

16 August 1962: Drummer Pete Best sacked. Irate fans hold demonstrations with placards saying 'Pete Forever, Ringo never' and local newspapers contain petitions for his reinstatement.

21 June 1963: John Lennon is reported in the papers to have beaten up Cavern DJ Bob Wooller at Paul McCartney's 21st birthday party, over a suggestion that Lennon had a sexual relationship with their homosexual manager Brian Epstein.

16 January 1964: The Beatles get a poor reception from the French press at the start of their season at the Paris Olympia.

4–30 June 1964: Ringo Starr is ill and has to be replaced on tour by Jimmy Nicol.

28 July 1964: Lennon and McCartney are almost electrocuted by faulty microphones at a concert in Sweden.

4 March 1966: John Lennon gives an interview in which he talks about the Beatles being more popular than Jesus. It is later reprinted in America, just before the start of the Beatles' US tour.

5 July 1966: Riot in Indonesia, after the Beatles allegedly snub Imelda Marcos.

1–12 August 1966: Religious groups in America burn Beatles records and books in protest at John Lennon's 'more popular than Jesus' remarks. Lennon is forced to apologise. At one point in their career, the American religious right alleged that the Beatles were part of a Communist plot. Dean Noebel of the 'Christian Crusade' claimed that 'The Communists have contrived an elaborate, calculating and scientific technique directed at rendering a generation of American youth useless through nerve-jangling mental deterioration and retardation.'

9 November 1966: Paul McCartney is involved in an accident while riding a moped. Rumours spread that he has been decapitated, giving rise to the 'Paul McCartney is dead' cult.

20 May 1967: The BBC bans *A Day in the Life* on the *Sgt Pepper* album for alleged drug references.

16 June 1967: Paul McCartney becomes the first Beatle to admit publicly to using LSD.

July 1967: *She's Leaving Home* on *Sgt Pepper* is condemned by the American religious right as coded support for abortion.

27 August 1967: Beatles manager Brian Epstein is found dead of a drug overdose at his Belgravia flat.

26 December 1967: *Magical Mystery Tour* is panned by the critics.

18 May 1968: Lennon convenes a meeting at Apple Corporation to tell the other members of the group not that he is more popular than Jesus, but that he *is* Jesus!

31 July 1968: Apple boutique – the most efficient way ever found of offsetting the profits made from the rest of the Beatles' empire – closes.

22 August 1968: Cynthia Lennon sues John for divorce, citing Yoko Ono. Divorce comes through the following November.

18 October 1968: John Lennon and Yoko Ono are raided for drugs while staying at Ringo Starr's Montague Square flat. Fined £150 for possession of cannabis.

3 February 1969: Start of break-up of Beatles' business empire, as three of the four appoint Allan Klein to sort out their affairs.

13 March 1969: George Harrison is raided for drugs.

16 May 1969: John Lennon is denied US visa, owing to his drugs conviction.

1 July 1969: John Lennon misses recording session, after a car crash.

25 November 1969: Lennon returns his MBE, in protest at Biafra, Vietnam – and his record *Cold Turkey* slipping down the charts.

31 December 1970: Paul McCartney starts proceedings in the High Court to wind up the Beatles' partnership.

CHAPTER 5

FROM PILKINGTON TO PYTHON: 1960s TELEVISION

There is little reality in this new serial which apparently we will have to suffer twice a week. This programme is doomed from the outset, with its dreary signature tune and grim scene of a row of terraced houses . . .

Ken Irwin, reviewing the new soap opera *Coronation Street* in the *Daily Mirror* in 1960

In July 1960 a Royal Commission was set up to look into the future of broadcasting. Its chairman, from whom it took its popular name, was an industrialist who had the one essential qualification for such a role: by his own admission Sir Harry Pilkington knew next to nothing about broadcasting. The Commission was prompted by the imminent ending of the BBC's charter and by pressures for a third channel. Pilkington was aided on the committee by Richard Hoggart, whose 1957 book *The Uses of Literacy* had been very hostile towards television and its effects on working class culture. In addition to assisting Pilkington on technical matters (such as 'What's that big glowing box in the corner?') Hoggart played a major role in drafting the Pilkington report. It will come as no surprise that the report was deeply critical of some aspects of broadcasting: 'From the representations which have been put to us, this is the underlying cause of disquiet about television; the belief, deeply felt, that the way television has portrayed human behaviour and treated moral issues has already done something and will in time do much to worsen the moral climate of the country.'

The report fired a useful shot across the bows of the commercial television companies in particular. Some of these felt that they had acquired a licence to print money (to use the unfortunate phrase coined by Lord Thompson in relation to his ownership of Scottish commercial

The way television has portrayed human behaviour and treated moral issues will in time do much to worsen the moral climate of the country

Richard Baker, doyen of television presenters.

These lucky children watched the Prince of Wales's Investiture on television.

Among the first television celebrity chefs were Fanny and Johnny Craddock.

television). The report called for a separation of programme-making on the one hand, and their broadcasting and the related sale of advertising on the other. (This did not happen until the formation of Channel 4 in 1982.) The BBC was given a comparatively clean bill of health by the Commission, and it was they who got the third channel, which opened in April 1964.

As the Television Bill worked its way through Parliament in March 1963, at least one other amateur critic used the opportunity provided by parliamentary privilege to make his views known. Donald Chapman, the Labour member for Birmingham Northfield, attacked what he called the television doldrums:

> For heaven's sake, let us do something about this peak period between 7.00 and 9.00 p.m. At the present, it is a terrible period. It is really shocking. I am not against fun and games on television. I like slapstick and I do not want to be thought of as a spoilsport, but we really have got into a terrible state when for years we have had this awful *Emergency Ward Ten*; *Double Your Money* and *Bootsie and Snudge*.

On target!

When you advertise on television you need
to be sure that your sales message is
aimed at the right audience at the right time.
You can be sure of a succession of direct hits
when you advertise on Associated-Rediffusion,
because the detailed information that we have about
the living, buying and viewing habits of our London
audience is at the disposal of all our advertisers.

✱ ASSOCIATED-REDIFFUSION
Television from London, Monday to Friday

Associated-Rediffusion Ltd., Television House, Kingsway, London, W.C.2. Tel: HOLborn 7888
also 61 Cornwall Street, Birmingham 3. Tel: Central 3041
also Queen's House, Queen Street, Manchester 2. Tel: Deansgate 7744

*Commercial television stations
advertised for advertisers – in the
newspapers?!*

Other MPs, recognising that a proposal to have television programming controlled by Parliament would be deeply unpopular, attacked his dictatorial attitude: 'There are hundreds and thousands of women who love *Emergency Ward Ten*. Try and knock that programme out and Mr Chapman will find he himself is knocked sideways.'

SPOILT FOR CHOICE

They televised a church service from Westminster Abbey on the eve of the opening of BBC2. This enabled those with the necessary equipment to compare the picture quality of the new 625 line system with the old 405 line system used up to that time, and the advance offered by the new format was very evident. The Archdeacon of Westminster used the opportunity to give a cheerfully up-beat sermon on the terrible responsibility facing broadcasters. It seemed the containment of nuclear weapons was not the only challenge facing their generation: 'Equally critical . . . is the power over the mind which techniques of mass communication, such as I am employing at this moment, have now thrust into the hands of fallible men. Power over the mind, when harnessed to wrong and unworthy ends, [can] undermine the foundations of society. The mass communicator takes upon himself a dreadful responsibility.' The Archdeacon pleaded for: 'That kind of integrity, that essential honesty, which despises the shoddy and the superficial. That a modern advertiser can assess our mental age to be about five and get away with it in sales and profits reflects little credit on him, but it is an even more terrible indictment of ourselves.'

Someone on high may have been listening to him, for the entire first night's broadcast on BBC2 was wiped out by a major power cut across much of London – the first night of broadcasts had to wait until the following evening. And how did the Corporation exercise its awesome power to manipulate our minds that night? There was *Playschool*, to indoctrinate the tiny tots; a programme in which Mr Ivor Cutler, a well-known eccentric, delivered a lecture on the history of electronic communications; a television version of the London stage musical success *Kiss Me Kate*; and a Russian comedian called Arkady Raikin. Our minds suitably adjusted, we all went to bed.

THE GREEN GREEN GRASS OF WIMBLEDON

The next great breakthrough came in July 1967, when Britain became the first European country to have colour television. The grass of Wimbledon turned from grey to green on our sets – no surprise there – and the kit worn by the contestants turned from white to, well, white . . . maybe tennis was not the best sporting event to show off colour television to its fullest advantage, after all.

Sets on which to view this spectacle were as rare as they had been when the first black and white services began before the war. It was estimated that there were only about 1,500 colour sets around on the first day of broadcasts, most of them in the hands of dealers. Even the newspaper television critics had to go to the BBC Television Centre to

Advertisers prepare for the new system.

see the new marvel of the age. Some of the available sets had been placed with men and women of influence by clever public relations operatives, and a number of the organisations supplied with them set up colour viewing parties.

It was not surprising that there had not been a flood of set buying, since they cost about the same as they did thirty years later – about £300 – though the average weekly wage at that time was less than £25. Renting was not much better. A rented set would cost you about 30s or more a week and the law demanded that you had to rent for a minimum of forty-two weeks, which meant an outlay of £60 or more. To add to the cost, the Postmaster General promised later in July to introduce a special £10 colour television licence from 1968. Quite apart from all this, large parts of the country could not even get colour – the Corporation's target was to reach 52 per cent of the population by 1970. By the end of the decade, the number of colour sets had risen to only 100,000.

Johnny Morris pioneered innovative animal programmes in the
1960s, though their real market was not always fully
understood by BBC executives.

Nor did you get much colour for your money, especially at first. Looking down the schedule for one day's programmes during the first week of colour broadcasting, the only programme shown as being in colour was *Late Night Sunday* – a review of last week's television, which – hang on a minute – had all been in black and white! It was promised that the colour content of programmes would rise to 15 to 25 hours per week by the end of the year, when the test period ended and the official service began. At least the colour itself was held to be good – better than the system used in America and Canada, and more restful on the eye than black and white.

But what were we all watching, back in those dear departed days? In the rest of this chapter we take a brief tour of 1960s television favourites.

UP YOUR STREET AND OTHER SOAPS

Granada Television decided in 1960 to launch *Florizel Street*, an experimental soap opera set in the back streets of a north-western city. There were hopes that the then current interest in things gritty and northern (this being the golden age of kitchen sink drama) would give it a head start, but nobody was betting their mortgage on it lasting beyond the initially planned thirteen episodes. The first episode went out in December of that year, but it was not until the following May that it was even broadcast across the whole ITV network. They had the characters worked out, but the name of the street was still not quite right. Agnes, the tea lady at Granada, told the management that Florizel sounded more like a disinfectant. So it was that Elsie Tanner (played by Pat Phoenix) became the femme fatale, not of Florizel but of Coronation Street. She was the street's woman with a past, not to mention a very active present and an eventful future, who was regarded by most of the other residents as no better than she ought to be.

By contrast, considerably better than she ought to be was the snooty landlady of the street's corner pub, the Rover's Return. Annie Walker (Doris Speed) had airs and graces above her station, and her long-suffering husband Jack (Arthur Leslie) was often the one to suffer when her ambitions were thwarted. In the snug of her establishment (in the days before it all became one bar) sat the three witches of Weatherfield, gathered around half-pint glasses for want of a cauldron and putting the world to rights with looks of disapproval that brought lip-pursing within the definition of grievous bodily harm. Their ringleader was a woman who could turn milk stout sour with a stare and who made the hairnet a fashion statement. Ena Sharples (Violet Carson) was ably abetted in her disapproval of just about everything by Martha Longhurst (Lynne Carol) and Minnie Caldwell (Margot Bryant).

The only current survivor of those early black and white days was the street's intellectual, Kenneth Barlow (played by William Roache) – then a callow schoolboy, but now a character rich in years, if not in wisdom, with enough of the vicissitudes of life under his fictional belt to last most people a dozen lifetimes. These days, residency in a soap opera has all the job security of football management, but many might still bet on young

Looks of disapproval that brought lip-pursing within the definition of grievous bodily harm

Master Barlow collecting his bus pass, if not his telegram from the Queen, as a resident of the Street.

The Street may have been the most successful and enduring of the 1960s soaps, but arguably the most prolific contributors to the genre were Hazel Adair and Peter Ling. They cut their teeth on *Compact*, a programme about a fictitious magazine of that name. The company's blurb at the time said it focused on 'the talented and temperamental people who worked on a topical magazine for the busy woman'. *Compact* had the unusual good fortune to be launched in 1962, during an Equity strike that put all the ITV soaps off the screen. Addicts of *Coronation Street* had no choice but to tune in to it for their fix of angst – and angst there was aplenty among the backstabbing and amorous staff. How they ever managed to publish so much as a handbill remains a mystery.

The series, which was criticised in some quarters as being too prissy and wholesome, finished in 1965, but Adair/Ling had moved on to their masterpiece. It was originally going to be called 'The Midland Road', its action being set in a Midlands motel at the fictitious King's Oak crossroads. But *Crossroads* it became, and millions of fans followed the drama, centred around proprietor Meg Richardson (Noele Gordon) and her staff and guests.

Even by the standards of soap characters, poor old Meg had something of a chequered existence at the motel. Her premises were blown up by a Second World War bomb; she was imprisoned for dangerous driving; her first lover left her for another; the second one tried to poison her; the first one came back and married her, and was promptly kidnapped by terrorists and died of a heart attack. The hotel then burnt to the ground. All that was missing were four or five mastectomies and a couple of alien abductions, and she would have experienced just about everything soap opera could throw at her.

Meg passed her luck on to her children. Son Sandy (Roger Tonge) got off relatively lightly, only being disabled in a motorbike accident (though nobody would have been surprised had they learned that the motorbike had fallen on him out of the sky). But it was Meg's daughter Jill (Jane Rossington) who really maintained the family tradition. She married a total of three times (once to a bigamist), had two miscarriages and only managed to give birth successfully on the occasion when her step-brother was the father. In the circumstances the fact that she also became a drug addict, an alcoholic and had a nervous breakdown can be regarded as no more than light relief.

Other figures who achieved cult status included the cleaner Amy Turtle (Ann George) and fashion icon Benny (Paul Henry), who found something to put inside a tea cosy that had a lower IQ than a tea pot. Considering that they broadcast a total of 4,510 episodes, it comes as little surprise to learn that it had something of a hurried production schedule. In fact, it came as a surprise to some that it had a production schedule at all – I thought they made it all up as they went along. But the episodes were churned out with relentless regularity, amid scenery that swayed like palm trees in a gale – and with all the continuity of an LSD trip. Regular viewers noted that the mole on the face of one actress migrated across her features from one episode to the next like a wandering beetle; that the

The fact that she also became a drug addict, an alcoholic and had a nervous breakdown can be regarded as no more than light relief

entire layout of the motel changed at one point, without the prior intervention of the building industry; and that Benny went out to fetch a spanner and disappeared entirely from the programme for six months (this last one may in fact have been quite plausible).

Predictably, the programme was savaged by the press. Even ATV's Head of Production, Bill Ward, was so embarrassed by it that he lobbied for it to be scrapped. It was not even fully networked until 1972, and only then in return for reducing the number of broadcasts from five to four a week, in an effort (vain, as it proved) to improve production values. But viewing figures, which at one point touched 17.6 million, were not to be denied. The motel eventually went through a series of owners. It ended up being converted into an emporium called Acorn Antiques

A sign of the times – the television version became more famous than the film.

and run by Victoria Wood, whose gifts as a soap star are woefully under-valued. However, despite her excellent efforts, this sequel was never quite as achingly funny as the original.

Other soaps enjoyed a more chequered career. *The Newcomers* uprooted a London family, the Coopers, and dumped them in the country town of Angleton. There they could share with the viewers all the loneliness and boredom of living on a new estate, not to mention the incomprehension of townies exposed to country life. Launched in 1965, the viewing public endured four years of loneliness, boredom and 'What's that green stuff coming out of the ground?'

There was plenty of green stuff in *United!*, the BBC's 1965 offering about Brentwich United, the bottom of Division 2 soccer team. The programme sought to combine sporting action with the domestic dramas of the team, and managed to please neither its male nor its female viewers in sufficient numbers. Despite securing the services of one Jimmy Hill (a well-known footballer of the day) as technical adviser, the series was shown the red card after two years.

HEROES AND VILLAINS

One of the most stylish – and stylised – adventure shows of the 1960s was *The Avengers*. This started life in 1960 as a conventional crime drama called *Police Surgeon*, with Patrick Macnee's John Steed initially playing second umbrella to Dr David Keel (whose part was taken by Ian Hendry).

She was played by Honor Blackman in a leather suit which was slightly smaller than her vital statistics

Hendry left in 1962 and Macnee/Steed took the lead role, as Cathy Gale joined the team. She was played by Honor Blackman in a leather suit which was, as I seem to recall fondly, slightly smaller than her vital statistics – a wardrobe mistake for which the men of Britain were hugely grateful. Gale and Steed capered through a series of adventures, defeating all sorts of bizarre villains with only the most stylised violence and absolutely no sex. The plots grew steadily more implausible and the creak of stressed leather ever more hypnotic, until Diana Rigg took over from Honor Blackman in 1965. She was cast in the role of Emma Peel, and was herself later replaced by Tara King (Linda Thorson).

The series was revived in the 1970s as *The New Avengers*. Steed was now joined by Purdey and Gambit (Joanna Lumley and Gareth Hunt). They tried to revive it as a feature film in the 1990s, with Ralph Fiennes in the Steed role, but expressions about sending a boy to do a man's job spring to mind – though definitely not in the case of Honor Blackman.

At the other end of the decade, equally surreal adventures were to be seen in the world of espionage, courtesy of *Department S*. There were conventional goodies among the agents, but the centrepiece was the playboy author Jason King (played by an elaborately coiffured Peter Wyngarde). King was apparently an amateur spy working for British intelligence. This was the only half-way plausible part of the plot, given that (on the evidence of our real intelligence services' performance during the 1960s), most of the real-life ones appeared to be rank amateurs. So successful was Jason King that he went on to get his own series in the early seventies.

The Saint was another well-heeled playboy, but he was more the conventional hero. The part was first offered to Patrick McGoohan, who apparently turned it down because it involved too much womanising. So sainthood was bestowed upon Roger Moore, a role that later helped earn him the position as James Bond. Moore had previously found fame on horseback, rather than in his famous yellow Volvo coupé, as the star of *Ivanhoe*. Before that, he had been a model for cardigans – some might say this was the acting role most suited to him.

The series was based on the Leslie Charteris books, which were written in the late 1920s. Moore played Simon Templar, a well-connected and well-heeled righter of wrongs, with no visible means of support and enough Brylcreem on his head to solve the oil crisis of the 1970s single-handedly. Claude Eustace Teal was the perpetually bewildered Scotland Yard detective, who arrived each week just in time to have our hero hand over the apprehended villain to him. The series ran for 118 episodes between 1963 and 1968.

For 1960s camp, you could not do much better than *Adam Adamant* (1966/67), in which Gerald Harper played Adam Llewellyn de Vere Adamant, an Edwardian adventurer who was put into suspended animation in 1902 by his arch-enemy 'The Face'. This leather-masked villain injected our hero with some kind of preservative drug (the formula to which is known today only by Cliff Richard) and froze him in a block of ice. Appropriately enough, he was thawed out in the era of television dinners, aged 99 but with the body of a 35-year-old. He soon acquired those essential accessories (a valet, Simms, and the dolly bird Georgina)

*The Saint, seen here on the left, with
antipodean crooner Frank Ifield.
Right: the Saint's famous car.*

with which to go swashbuckling anew. The series provided an interesting juxtaposition between the values and language of the Edwardians and the brash world of the mods:

'Not dancing, Adam?'

'Not while my country is at stake!'

Among those who directed these gems was a young Ridley Scott.

Much more at the cutting edge of modern technology was *The Man from UNCLE*. Those who thought of it as a cheap, tongue-in-cheek rip-off of the James Bond format may be surprised to know that Bond's creator, Ian Fleming, was also marginally involved in this caper. He and the producer Norman Felton conceived the idea over lunch, and it was Fleming who suggested the name Solo for one of its lead characters, based on a minor figure in one of his own novels. It was only at the insistence of the Bond movie producers that Fleming dropped out of any closer involvement in the project.

Behind the apparently innocent facade of Del Floria's dry cleaning and tailoring repair shop in downtown Manhattan lay the headquarters of UNCLE (the United Network Command for Law Enforcement), sworn to defend the world against the evil plans of THRUSH (Technological Hierarchy for the Removal of Undesirables and the Subjugation of Humanity – just thank your lucky stars they weren't called LESSER SPOTTED HEATHLAND WOODPECKER, or we could have been here all night).

From their vast, humming seat of technology, agents Napoleon Solo (Robert Vaughn) and Ilya Kuryakin (David McCallum) were dispatched each week to save the world by the wise old boss of UNCLE, Alexander Waverly (Leo G. Carroll). Invariably they were unable to do so without the intervention of scantily clad, nubile young women – a problem that has bedevilled film heroes for years. They saved the world a total of ninety-nine times and the series also spawned eight feature films. At its

An early version of pay per view.

height the programme had a fan club of some 500,000 members. Film stars fell over themselves to get in on the action and the list of guest stars included Sharon Tate, Vincent Price, Joan Collins, Nancy Sinatra, Sonny and Cher, Joan Crawford, Telly Savalas, Terry-Thomas and a pre-*Star Trek* William Shatner and Leonard Nimoy.

But perhaps the weirdest and most improbable cult of the decade grew up around the series conceived by, and starring, Patrick McGoohan. Astonishingly, only seventeen episodes of *The Prisoner* were ever made. McGoohan played a former secret agent who was kidnapped, imprisoned, renamed Number 6 and questioned about his past in a weird Welsh village (actually Portmeirion, the creation of eccentric architect Clough Williams-Ellis. The village is still dining out on the association with the television show, thirty years later.) Those who were expecting an explanation of all the mystery in the last episode were doomed to disappointment, though years of analysis suggest that it might contain some kind of message about the Vietnam War. It was repeated in 1976 and 1983/4; on the latter occasion, the television company ran one of the episodes in the wrong order, without realising it. It was that kind of programme.

THE SATIRE BOOM –
THAT WAS THE WEEK THAT WAS

Satire enjoyed one of its periodic revivals in the 1960s, following the success of *Beyond the Fringe* in the 1961 Edinburgh Festival. Peter Cook opened his Establishment Club and *Private Eye* was founded in the same year. When Hugh Greene set up the television satire show *That Was The Week That Was* (generally shortened to TW3) he gave it to Current Affairs, rather than Light Entertainment, in an effort to sharpen it up. Ned Sherrin was made the director. The show enjoyed an influence and notoriety that belied its relatively short life. It changed social habits to the extent that people used to leave the pub early on Saturday nights to go home and watch it.

TW3 was presented by a youthful David Frost (and anything that makes him look like a threat to the Establishment does seem an awfully long time ago). Also featured were Roy Kinnear, Lance Percival, Willie Rushton and Bernard Levin, with Millicent Martin providing the songs. One of its contributors was a graduate of the University of Life, rather than of Oxbridge. This was Frankie Howerd, who said of the programme 'These days, you can't be filthy unless you've got a degree.' No less distinguished was the list of writers and researchers who contributed, including Labour front bencher Gerald Kaufmann and future Scottish Secretary Ian Lang, along with better-known writers Christopher Booker, Peter Schaffer, Keith Waterhouse and Willis Hall, John Braine, Kenneth Tynan and Dennis Potter.

The show was launched to rapturous acclaim and violent abuse in equal proportions, sometimes from the same newspaper. The *Daily Telegraph*, for example, spoke of it as raising 'questions of fairness, propriety and even libel' and saying that it 'enabled its script-writers to disseminate personal abuse, and bitter attacks upon authority of every kind', all of

It 'enabled its script-writers to disseminate personal abuse, and bitter attacks upon authority of every kind'

which sounds like a pretty good definition of satire to me. The same paper also concluded: 'Without reservations, TW3, the BBC's first late night satirical show, is brilliant . . . for the first time it seems reasonable that one should need a licence for a television set – it can be as lethal as a gun.'

Within three weeks of its launch, the Postmaster General was calling for prior sight of its scripts. He was very firmly warned off by Prime Minister Harold Macmillan, in a memorandum which only became public during the 1990s, under the Thirty Year Rule: 'I hope that you will not, repeat not, take any action about "That Was The Week That Was" without consulting me. It is a good thing to be laughed over – it is better than to be ignored.'

The show attacked all sorts of targets that the BBC guidelines had hitherto deemed out of bounds, such as religion (their *Which?* style guide to comparative religion concluded that the Church of England was 'a jolly good little faith for a very moderate outlay' and made it their Best Buy); the royal family (Ian Lang's commentator happily describing the details of the royal family's outfits as the royal barge sank and they all disappeared beneath the waves); and Members of Parliament (Gerald Kaufmann's piece on the silent thirteen – those MPs who had been in the House for more than ten years without once speaking. One of these later broke the habit of a lifetime by raising a complaint about the item in the House – apparently it was even funnier than the original broadcast). Not even dear old Dixon of Dock Green was safe. He was shown entering a room, beating the stuffing out of a suspect and saying 'Just a routine enquiry, sir', as he raised his hand in salute, stepped over the bleeding victim and departed.

Mary Whitehouse hated it. She described it as: 'The epitome of what's wrong with the BBC – anti-authority, anti-religious, anti-patriotism, pro-dirt and poorly produced, yet having the support of the Corporation and apparently impervious to discipline from within or disapproval from without.' The show was dropped, despite the fact that it was attracting viewing figures of twelve million for a late night show in 1964. This also happened to be the year the BBC's charter came up for renewal and there was a general election in the offing. I would like to tell you that there was no connection between these facts, but you might think I was being satirical.

The epitome of what's wrong with the BBC – anti-authority, anti-religious, anti-patriotism, pro-dirt and poorly produced

GRITTY REALISM

If further evidence were needed that programmes like *Dixon of Dock Green*, along with their model policemen and deferential ('It's a fair cop, you got me bang to rights, guv') villains were history, the more earthily realistic *Z Cars* became the biggest television cop show of the 1960s. It was born from an earlier (1961) programme *Jacks and Knaves*, based on the exploits of a Liverpool detective, Sergeant William Prendergast. The idea came to producer Troy Kennedy Martin when he was confined to bed with the mumps. To pass the time, he tuned his radio to the local police waveband and was struck by the difference between what he heard and the police programmes of the day. The police were often no longer

Some 1960s big screen and television favourites – actress and railway child Jenny Agutter, actor George Cole, and comedians Terry Scott and Jack Douglas.

operating in established working class communities where everybody knew everyone else. In many areas they were having to deal with the anonymity of the new high-rise estates which, apart from all their other problems, were proving to be breeding grounds for crime. The new programme's opening scene was the grave of a young police constable, killed in the line of duty. It was his death that led to the formation of a vehicle patrol – instead of bobbies on the beat – from which comes the series name.

Z Cars was filmed in the fair Liverpool suburb of Kirkby which, by the use of advanced camera trickery, was transformed into the grim and fictitious northern city of Newtown. It was made initially with the co-operation of the Lancashire Police, and was often based on case material supplied by former policemen. However, that support disappeared when policemen began to be portrayed as mere mortals, drinking, gambling, arguing and, in one controversial episode, beating their wives. Viewers – and even Jack Warner himself, the actor who played Dixon of Dock Green – also complained at this realistic treatment of the police. But it was not realistic enough for Troy Kennedy Martin, who wanted to show the police losing the battle over crime sometimes. He soon left the show, unable to dissuade the company from the idea that the police always get their man.

The show ran for over 650 episodes between 1962 and 1978 and spawned a number of offshoots, such as *Softly, Softly* and *Barlow at Large*. The cast-lists read like a *Who's Who* of British television, and include such future stars as John Thaw, Leonard Rossiter, Judi Dench, Alison Steadman and Joss Ackland. Among its other claims to fame, its theme music *Johnny Todd* went into the top ten in 1962 and was adopted as the theme tune for Everton Football Club.

Even more startlingly real was *The War Game*. This groundbreaking 1965 programme used cinema verité and grainy black and white film to try to capture the true horror of a nuclear attack on modern Britain. So realistic did it seem at the time, and so far removed from the 'chin up and be cheerful' school of civil defence documentary, that Hugh Greene banned it from our screens. It was not seen by television audiences until 1985, on the fortieth anniversary of Hiroshima.

LAUGH? 1960s COMEDY

Seen in retrospect the 1960s look like a golden era for television comedy. One show which must take a great deal of the credit for this was *Comedy Playhouse*, which provided a platform for a wealth of humour. The driving forces behind it included writers Alan Simpson and Ray Galton, who had previously written much of Tony Hancock's material, and whose contribution to the series was the pilot programme that was to become *Steptoe and Son*. Among the other shows launched as one-off trials from *Comedy Playhouse* were *All Gas and Gaiters*, *Till Death Us Do Part*, *Me Mammy*, *Not in Front of the Children*, *The Liver Birds*, *Last of the Summer Wine*, *Happy Ever After* and *Open All Hours*.

The success of the revue *Beyond the Fringe* gave us another enduring comedy duo – Pete and Dud (Peter Cook and Dudley Moore). Their

Jack Warner who played Dixon of Dock Green also complained at this realistic treatment of the police

Morecombe . . . and Wisdom?
Eric Morecombe, unusually paired
with another popular comedian of
the day, Norman Wisdom.

dialogues around the bar table might encompass such subjects as the royal family (an imagined diary for the Queen – 'Opened Parliament; went to the toilet' . . . her day seemed to involve a great many comfort breaks) or fine art (speculation on the little piece of gauze that always flutters down to hide the model's embarrassment just at the moment the artist is painting that part of her). But their discussions were invariably marked by the contrast between earthy vulgarity and grandiloquent flights of fancy. The Pete character in particular was a man who would have been engrossed by the superfluousness of his own verbosity, if only he'd had the faintest idea what it meant.

Other series ranged from the more traditionally affectionate lampoon of the Walmington-on-Sea Home Guard, in *Dad's Army*, through to the attempt to recreate the eccentric world of *Express* newspaper columnist Beachcomber by Spike Milligan, in *The World of Beachcomber*. But it was another show that really captured the imagination of the 1960s comedy viewer.

Monty Python's Flying Circus hit our screens in 1969, and proved to be one of the most inventive and certainly the best-known of the new comedies of the decade. Barry Took initiated the idea, originally as a late night satire show. Its popularity very quickly saw it move from BBC2 to BBC1 and into an earlier slot. But *Python* did not spring fully formed from the fevered brains of its creators. A number of earlier shows can justly claim to have prepared the way for it. John Cleese made a few early appearances on TW3 (above) and both he and other *Python* members wrote for *The Frost Report*. But much more influential was the *At Last the 1948 Show*, which appeared two years before Python.

The *1948 Show* included Pythons Cleese and Chapman, along with Marty Feldman and Tim Brooke-Taylor. David Frost produced it. It anticipated *Python*'s use of a continuity announcer, but instead of John Cleese's 'And now for something completely different' it had the delightfully vacuous Aimi Macdonald, who linked the items with little tableaux and pronouncements of truly epic banality.

Some of its sketches were genuinely surreal: Graham Chapman's solo wrestler, trying to strangle himself, or the dentist who climbs into his patient's mouth and carries out the extraction with the aid of dynamite. In another, a cabaret singer has a gunman hidden under her voluminous

Marty Feldman, seen here in a charity football match.

dress and carries on with her number while he stages a shoot-out with the encircling police. The police try to send a priest in to talk him out, but the fugitive cries out from beneath the petticoats 'Go back! This is no place for a priest!' In yet another sketch, wartime bomber pilots are sent out on a mission without radios – they are issued with foreign change to use the phone to keep in touch – and with seriously out-of-date maps. They have to fly over Gaul and drop the bombs on the Holy Roman Empire, just under the G of Visigoths. Marty Feldman is particularly memorable for the intensely irritating characters he used to play – the man in the bookshop who is looking for *David Coperfield* – not the Dickens one with two 'p's, but the Edmund Wells version – 'much more thorough'. He was also the man in the railway carriage who gets an unwilling John Cleese to play 'I spy' – would you have guessed that 'E' was for 'ectoplasm'?

At about the same time, there was also the series *Do Not Adjust Your Set*. This brought to our screens Pythons Eric Idle, Terry Jones and Michael Palin, along with Denise Coffey, David Jason and the Bonzo Dog Doodah Band. One of the features of this show was the character Captain Fantastic, played by David Jason, who was locked in permanent battle with his nemesis Mrs Black (Denise Coffey). Finally, at just about the time that *Python* was emerging, Palin and Jones made *The Complete and Utter History of Britain*, all of it compressed into six thirty-minute episodes.

AUNTY GOES POP

How did the television companies respond to the important new teenage market? The first ever pop programme had been on the commercial side. *Cool for Cats*, launched at the very end of 1956, simply had dancers interpreting pop records. *Juke Box Jury* came in during the last months of the 1950s, with the suave David Jacobs inviting a panel to vote new releases a hit or a miss. This idea was shamelessly stolen by the other side as 'Spin a Disc', one of the features in *Thank Your Lucky Stars* which was launched in 1961 to counter the popularity of *Juke Box Jury*. They added the refinement of a sixteen-year-old clerk named Janice Nicholls, whose catch-phrase 'Oi'll give eet foive!' briefly entered the national consciousness. It was the first programme to give the Beatles national television exposure, in February 1963, but *Juke Box Jury* got the Beatles as their entire panel in December of the same year, and later extended the jury box to accommodate all five Rolling Stones.

One of the BBC's early efforts sounded more like a programme about carpet cleaning. *Beat and Shake* promised 'twenty-five minutes of non-stop beat and shake'. After a brief life on BBC2 it was transformed into *Gadzooks! It's All Happening* which itself became *Gadzooks! It's the in-crowd*, which in turn became shortened to, you guessed it, *Gadzooks!* It appeared that the BBC was being run by somebody who had not listened to any teenage slang since the fifteenth century.

You got the impression in other ways that Aunty BBC did not quite get the hang of this teenage business. 1964 saw the introduction of their most durable pop vehicle. It was based on a radio programme of the day, broadcast on the old Light programme, called *Pick of the Pops*. The original set was modelled on a coffee bar disco, and the presenters sat in front of record turntables, while the artistes mimed to top twenty hits. After the Musicians' Union banned miming in 1966, artistes had either to pre-record their song for the show or play it live. Where acts were not available to appear, dance groups like Pan's People or Legs and Co. performed to the record and Mary Whitehouse duly phoned in to complain about them.

The main problem with *Top of the Pops* was its early presenters. Jimmy Savile was hardly a character that teenagers could identify with, since he was pushing forty by the time he started presenting it. But at least with his dyed platinum (sometimes tartan) hair and outlandish dress sense, you could fool yourself into thinking that he came from another planet. But David Jacobs, Alan Freeman and Pete Murray – consummate professionals though they may have been – were worse than from another planet. They were from another generation! It was as embarrassing as having a trendy dad! Youthful tokenism appeared in the form of Samantha Juste, who put the records on for them.

Even ITV's best-known contribution to the genre, *Ready, Steady, Go!*, had a similar problem. This programme, which went out on Friday nights, announcing that 'the weekend starts here', was more adventurous in its selection of acts, and became the showcase for mod fashions. If asked to name its presenter, you would probably recall the young mod Cathy McGowan. She originally replied to an advertisement from the programme, looking for a typical teenager to advise them on the consumer appeal of the show. Her potential was spotted and she was soon pushed out in front of the cameras. The audience could identify with her and her occasional lapses into amateurism, but few now remember the grey-suited presence of Keith Fordyce as the main presenter. This refugee from *Housewives Choice* and *Family Favourites* would have needed a very dark night indeed to pass as a teenager. It was a bit like Pan's People or Legs and Co. being followed by the formation ballroom dancing team from the Twilight Home.

WHILE ON THE RADIO, WE WERE WORRIED ABOUT JIM . . .

The late 1960s saw the end of a national institution that had been running since the start of 1948. *Mrs Dale's Diary* was the story of a middle class family, Dr Jim Dale and his wife Mary, who lived in the comfortable south London suburb of Parkwood Hill. The trivia of their lives flowed effortlessly over the dramas of the real world. Aliens could have taken over the Hill, but Mrs Dale would still have been preoccupied with the question of who was going to do the flower arranging in the church next week. The Queen Mother used to listen avidly to Mrs Dale. She is reported to have said: 'It is the only way of knowing what goes on in a middle class family.' 'What went on' included living in a sort of peculiar time warp. This manifested itself, for example, in the twins still sleeping in cots, eating in high chairs and otherwise being treated as helpless tots some three-and-a-half years after their radio 'birth'.

In February 1962 some programme executive made the fatal error of uprooting the Dales from Parkwood Hill to the relatively gritty reality of the East Anglian new town of Exton. Things were never quite the same thereafter. The family was torn from its staple diet of domestic bliss and forced to confront current issues, such as racial intolerance, the menopause, sex (the earlier twins were no doubt the result of immaculate conception) and even homosexuality (a term Mrs Dale probably had to look up in a dictionary). 'The Dales', as they were by then known, were axed in April 1969, despite huge protests and (as it turned out, unfulfilled) threats to resurrect them on independent radio. The nearest 'The Dales' came to being revived was when two of their episodes were pirated by Radio Caroline. I blame the move to Exton. Without that, we could even today have been listening to the twins, sucking contentedly on their dummies in their high chairs as they looked forward to their fiftieth birthdays.

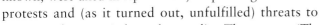
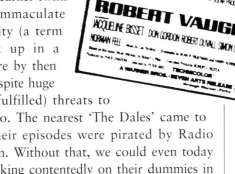

FILMS: THE BEST AND THE REST

Some people in the 1960s were still tearing themselves away from the television and going to the cinemas. Among the main attractions were these winners of Academy Awards for best film in the 1960s:

1960 *Ben Hur*
1961 *The Apartment*
1962 *West Side Story*
1963 *Lawrence of Arabia*
1964 *Tom Jones*
1965 *My Fair Lady*
1966 *The Sound of Music*
1967 *A Man for all Seasons*
1968 *In the Heat of the Night*
1969 *Oliver!*

and some of the also-rans:

1960 *The Magnificent Seven, Psycho*
1961 *El Cid, La Dolce Vita*
1962 *A Kind of Loving, Doctor No*
1963 *Cleopatra, The Birds*
1964 *Doctor Strangelove, Mary Poppins*
1965 *Repulsion, Doctor Zhivago*
1966 *Who's Afraid of Virginia Woolf?*
1967 *Camelot, Bonnie and Clyde*
1968 *The Lion in Winter, 2001*
1969 *Oh! What a Lovely War, Midnight Cowboy, Easy Rider, Butch Cassidy and the Sundance Kid.*

CHAPTER 6

WHITE HEAT: 1960s POLITICS

I never thought I could be brought down by two tarts.
                    Harold Macmillan, on his resignation

The contrasts between the prime ministers with which Britain started and ended the 1960s illustrate the changes which took place in the decade. Harold Macmillan came across as the Edwardian amateur. Bernard Levin likened his presentation to 'a down-at-heel actor, resting between engagements at the decrepit theatres of minor provincial towns'. But behind his sometimes bumbling appearance there was a keen mind and, as he was to show in July 1962, a steely ruthlessness. By contrast Harold Wilson was a trained economist and the first premier to be born after the start of the First World War; he was keenly aware of the growing power of the media and was skilled in its exploitation. He seemed much more at home in the age of the 'white heat of technology' that was then being ushered in.

Macmillan's decline and fall can be traced back to early 1961, when Chancellor Selwyn Lloyd introduced an unpopular budget in response to a slowdown in the economy. He followed this by further increases in taxation and public spending cuts later in the year. The government also became involved in interventionist state planning, through the introduction of the National Economic Development Council, or 'Neddy'. This was a complete reversal of the emphasis on individual freedom that ran through Macmillan's 'one nation' brand of Conservatism. Add to this a series of embarrassing spy scandals and the staleness that comes from a long period in government, and their popularity began to slide alarmingly.

A series of by-elections started to go against them, most spectacularly in March 1962, when the Liberals turned a Conservative majority of 14,760 in the safe suburban Kent seat of Orpington into a Liberal majority of 7,855. The term 'Orpington man' came to represent the hordes of disillusioned Conservative voters said to inhabit suburbia up and down the country. In July of the same year the Conservatives found themselves pushed down into third place in a by-election at Leicester North East. The following day saw what was called the July massacre, when Super Mac became Mac the Knife, sacking half his cabinet at a stroke. The sackings

The term 'Orpington man' came to represent the hordes of disillusioned Conservative voters

appeared to be random. The left and right wings of the party were equally savaged and there was no evidence that anti-Macmillan plotters were being culled. The Lord Chancellor, the Chancellor of the Exchequer, the Ministers for Education, Defence, Housing and Local Government and others all got the chance to spend more time with their families.

Few were impressed with this move, apart from those who secretly admired its ruthlessness. Harold Wilson said he had got rid of the wrong half of the Cabinet and Jeremy Thorpe coined his famous phrase about Macmillan laying down his friends for his life. Within his own party, shocked colleagues felt he was 'making enemies on a grand scale' and the general public thought it smacked of vindictiveness. Moreover, Macmillan now looked increasingly out of place in a reshuffled Cabinet that was for the most part very much younger than himself. The dismissed Lord Chancellor, Lord Kilmuir, complained about the manner of his dismissal, after eleven years in the job, saying that a cook would have been given more notice: 'Ah, yes,' replied Macmillan, 'But good cooks are hard to find.' The worst was yet to come for Macmillan. During the Profumo scandal, his judgement was called into question for being too ready to accept the word of a Cabinet colleague. Macmillan resigned, ostensibly due to prostate trouble, in October 1963.

HOME, SWEET HOME

The selection of Macmillan's successor also marked the passing of another traditional way of doing things within the Conservative party. Their leaders had always been chosen by an arcane process of consultation among the various echelons of the party. Thus it had been in 1957, when Macmillan had usurped the heir apparent, R.A. Butler. In 1963 it was generally held that there were at least four serious runners for the Prime Minister's job – Reginald Maudling, Iain Macleod, Edward Heath and Quentin Hogg (aka Lord Hailsham). Hailsham was able to stand because of the Peerage Act, passed earlier that same year, which allowed peers to renounce their peerages in pursuit of their political ambitions. This Act had become law partly through the campaign of a man who would most definitely not feature in this particular leadership battle – Viscount Stansgate, better known later as Labour Cabinet Minister Tony Benn.

After a mysterious process of consultation which involved the Cabinet, the parliamentary party, the Lords and the constituencies, and which even an insider like Reginald Maudling did not understand, Macmillan switched his support from Quentin Hogg to a hitherto completely unfancied outsider. Hailsham and Maudling tried to unite the party by standing down in favour of Rab Butler, but to no avail. Macmillan was determined to block Butler's candidature. Out of the leadership contest emerged one of the most improbable Prime Ministers of modern times – the Earl of Home.

Home (pronounced Hume, just as 'trousers' are pronounced 'trisers' in his circle) was said to have had the classic education for a Conservative Prime Minister of his generation: Eton, Oxford, Munich and Suez. He had

One of the most improbable Prime Ministers of modern times

Reginald Maudling (standing), one of the Tory leadership hopefuls defeated by Sir Alec Douglas-Home.

been secretary to Neville Chamberlain, Commonwealth Relations Secretary under Eden, Macmillan's Foreign Secretary and had played cricket for Middlesex. However, he had previously dismissed himself as a possible candidate for the post on the grounds that he had to do all his sums with matchsticks. As he candidly put it: 'I never understood a word about economics. If I had thought I was going to be Prime Minister, I would have taken more trouble to understand the various theories.' He also had little experience of domestic government, except in the direct, hands-on sense that he owned rather a lot of Scotland. At the time of his elevation to Prime Minister, he had 96,000 acres of farmland, forest and grouse moor to his name, complete with 56 tenant farmers.

Harold Wilson had great fun with both the process and its outcome. The Tories, he said, had 350 Members of Parliament and could not find a single leader among them. Instead, they had opted for an aristocrat, unelected and with no idea of the day-to-day problems of ordinary people. As he put it: 'After half a century of democratic advance, the whole process has ground to a halt with a fourteenth Earl.'

Home's daughter, Lady Caroline Douglas-Home, leapt stoutly, if not wisely, to daddy's defence: 'He is used to dealing with estate workers. I cannot see how anyone can say he is out of touch.' Wilson's description of the new Prime Minister as an 'elegant anachronism' and his repeated references to Sir Alec (as he became on renouncing his title) as 'the fourteenth Earl' prompted Home to point out that Harold was presumably the fourteenth Mr Wilson. It was possibly the only good blow Home ever landed on him.

Political rivals in the 1960s: Sir Alec Douglas-Home (above right) and Harold Wilson.

Home's selection as the leader of a supposedly 'one nation' party was an extraordinary misjudgement at a time when traditional deference to the aristocracy was well and truly on the wane and the cult of the working class hero was being born. Even some of his own supporters despaired of the choice: 'We are sick of seeing old-looking men dressed in flat caps and bedraggled tweeds, stalking with a 12-bore.' He was not helped, in an increasingly televisual age, by an unfortunate screen persona that made him look like a speaking skull. Although popular in the party (it was said that he brought out the maternal instinct in Conservative ladies of the day), and many people underestimated his abilities, he was not an electoral asset.

Even so, he lost the 1964 election by the smallest of margins. Harold Wilson and Labour got in with an overall majority of just four seats. It is said that if just 900 voters had abstained or voted the other way Labour would have lost the election. One of the factors which cost Labour dear was the postal vote (introduced, ironically, by the Attlee government). It has always worked against them and, without it, it was estimated that Labour might have had a majority of between twenty and forty seats.

The election was a close call in another way. The very day it took place, the Russian leader Nikita Kruschchev was being overthrown in a palace coup in Moscow. News of the coup did not spread through Britain until after the polls had closed. Had word got round just a few hours earlier, it is thought that it would have led to a rush of voters opting for the familiar safety of the Conservatives, rather than a Labour party untried in foreign policy since 1951. (On such chance matters do elections turn. In 1959 it was alleged that Clint Eastwood cost Labour the election. Labour usually turn out a significant part of the vote at about 7.00 p.m. but on this occasion ITV chose that time to launch a new western series called *Rawhide* and starring Mr Eastwood. It appears he frustrated the best efforts of many a Labour canvasser.)

Home finally resigned in July 1965, shortly after an opinion poll showed him lagging behind Wilson in every department, including sincerity. It is surely nature's way of telling you to go, when you come second in the sincerity stakes to Harold Wilson, whose career was described as 'an undeviating lack of candour'. Wilson was a man of whom it was said:

How can you tell if Harold Wilson is lying?

His lips are moving.

Edward Heath – the first democratically chosen leader of the Conservatives.

Home was to be the last twentieth-century Prime Minister to come from an aristocratic background. Wilson, who succeeded him, was a product of the grammar school system and claimed to have been a barefoot youngster. (Macmillan was not the first to suggest that, if Wilson had ever gone barefoot, it was because he had been too big for his boots.) But Home left the Conservatives one important legacy – a new method of choosing their leader. His own appointment had looked particularly shabby and lacking in moral authority, especially when compared with Wilson's open election by his parliamentary party after the death of Hugh Gaitskell. This time Home ensured that the Conservatives had a similarly transparent process, which gave them Edward Heath as their next leader. The method did not guarantee success, however; by February 1966 Heath's popularity ratings were lower even than Home's had been.

BABBLING BROOKE AND BIBULOUS BROWN

The remainder of this chapter looks at two very prominent, and very different, politicians from the 1960s. One of them had human failings that contributed to his being one of the most popular political figures of the decade. The failings of the other had quite the opposite effect.

Henry Brooke

When Harold Wilson said that Macmillan had got rid of the wrong half of his Cabinet, one of the people he had in mind may have been Home Secretary R.A. Butler, whom he replaced with Henry Brooke. Even by the modest standards of Home Secretaries of the day, Henry Brooke was subsequently regarded as a disaster in the post. He was described as 'accident-prone' by his few apologists and as 'dishonest', 'inhumane' and 'totally lacking in sensitivity', or worse, by everybody else. Marcus Lipton MP called him 'the most hated man in Britain'. TW3's regular attacks on him – however vicious – would always end with the cod disclaimer: 'Seriously though, he's doing a grand job'.

Brooke started his political career with characteristic wrongheadedness. He spoke in the following glowing terms of our wartime leader to the Commons in 1940: 'The men who win wars are the men with burning hearts and cool heads. . . . It is because I see that combination present in the Prime Minister that I would rather trust him to lead us to victory than any other man.' Unfortunately for him, the Prime Minister he was referring to was Neville Chamberlain, and he thereby consigned himself to the political wilderness for the war years. He lost his seat in the Labour landslide of 1945, only to be reselected for the safe seat of Hampstead in 1950.

Within his first week as Home Secretary, he announced that he was going to deport a West Indian girl for stealing less than £2 worth of groceries (her first offence). He said: 'I think it would be a great act of injustice if I were to stand in the way of her returning to Jamaica.' She spent six weeks in prison, awaiting deportation, until Brooke was

'Seriously though, he's doing a grand job'

Nuclear power – and the fear of it – dominated the 1960s. Civil defence remained a preoccupation during the decade. (The main victim in the top picture seems to be the lady's hair-do.) Purveyors of nuclear power spoke highly of it, while insurers disavowed any responsibility for it. Even God was called upon to take a position on it.

A partnership has been established between The Nuclear Power Plant Company Limited and The AEI–John Thompson Nuclear Energy Company Limited to design and construct better and cheaper nuclear power stations

This new enterprise is called

The Nuclear Power Group

and combines the research, development, manufacturing and construction resources of these industrial concerns of world-wide renown.

ASSOCIATED ELECTRICAL INDUSTRIES LIMITED

CLARKE, CHAPMAN AND COMPANY LIMITED

ALEX. FINDLAY AND COMPANY LIMITED

HEAD, WRIGHTSON AND COMPANY LIMITED

SIR ROBERT McALPINE AND SONS LIMITED

C. A. PARSONS AND COMPANY LIMITED

A. REYROLLE AND COMPANY LIMITED

STRACHAN AND HENSHAW LIMITED

JOHN THOMPSON LIMITED

WHESSOE LIMITED

RADBROKE HALL · KNUTSFORD · CHESHIRE

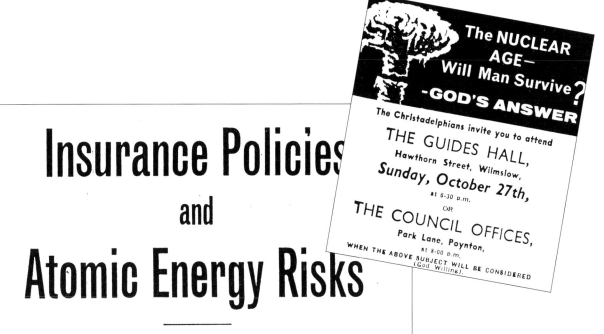

The NUCLEAR AGE— Will Man Survive? —GOD'S ANSWER

The Christadelphians invite you to attend

THE GUIDES HALL,
Hawthorn Street, Wilmslow,
Sunday, October 27th,
at 6-30 p.m.

OR

THE COUNCIL OFFICES,
Park Lane, Poynton,
at 8-00 p.m.
WHEN THE ABOVE SUBJECT WILL BE CONSIDERED
(God Willing).

Insurance Policies
and
Atomic Energy Risks

Announcement by the
BRITISH INSURANCE ASSOCIATION and LLOYD'S

All new insurance policies which relate to the various forms of material damage to property on land or liability to third parties will, as from 1st April 1960, contain a clause making it clear that any injury to any person or any damage to any property arising out of ionising radiations or contamination by radioactivity emanating from nuclear fuel or nuclear waste is not insured. The clause will be added to existing policies as they come up for renewal on or after the same date.

If an escape of radioactivity from an atomic installation covered by licence should occur, anyone who is injured or suffers damage to his property will be entitled by virtue of the Nuclear Installations (Licensing and Insurance) Act, 1959 to be compensated by the operator of the installation concerned. The operator will be enabled through special insurance facilities provided by the British Insurance (Atomic Energy) Committee to meet such claims for compensation. In these circumstances it will not, therefore, be necessary or indeed possible for the general public to insure against loss from this cause.

The clause does not extend to exclude other sources of ionising radiations such as radioisotopes, X-ray machines and particle accelerators. Those who use them in industry,

agriculture, medicine, research and other fields will still be able to obtain the insurances they require.

The exclusion will not in general apply to life, pension, personal accident or sickness insurances. Policies covering the liabilities of employers to employees for personal injuries sustained in the course of their work will remain generally unaffected. Motor policies will be endorsed but the motorist's liability under the Road Traffic Acts will be fully provided for. The position under marine and aviation insurances is still under consideration.

The British Insurance (Atomic Energy) Committee was set up in August 1956 to mobilise the resources of the whole of the British Insurance market, comprising Tariff, Independent and Mutual Companies and Lloyd's Underwriters and can provide insurance cover to the operators of nuclear installations in respect of their liability to the public in accordance with the Nuclear Installations (Licensing and Insurance) Act, 1959. The Committee does not, however, provide insurance against damage or injury caused by radioactive fall-out from the explosion of nuclear bombs or similar nuclear devices.

Henry Brooke, quite possibly surrounded by his entire fan club.

persuaded otherwise. He also barred comedian Lenny Bruce from working in Britain and tried to ban the entry of American Nazi leader George Lincoln Rockwell – two days after he had actually arrived. When a convicted spy, Robert Soblen, escaped from prison in America and fled to Britain, Brooke announced his intention to deport him back to the States, even though the American government had not even asked him to do so. Soblen managed to evade deportation by the rather extreme step of committing suicide, but Brooke, not to be thwarted, sent the body back. On another occasion, Brooke made a parliamentary statement in which he claimed that the former French Prime Minister Georges Bidault had been refused entry to the country – just as Bidault was giving an interview to British television on British soil. Brooke was also implicated in a cover-up involving some corrupt policemen, whose victims spent a year in prison. In the case of the African dissident Chief Anthony Enahoro, Brooke stood accused of sending him back to certain imprisonment and possible death in Nigeria.

This dismal record led to one of the most curious episodes of the 1966 General Election, when campaigners of all political colours united to get Brooke voted out of Parliament. A huge canvassing effort within his constituency succeeded in achieving one of the biggest swings seen in the elections of the 1960s. A large Conservative majority was overturned and Brooke, rewarded for his incompetence with a life peerage, was consigned to the relative safety of the House of Lords.

George Brown

When Harold Wilson won the leadership of the Labour party in February 1963, his opponents were James Callaghan (later himself to enjoy a spell as Labour Prime Minister) and George Brown. Whether a Labour government led by George Brown would have been better or worse than the one we got (and whether Labour under George Brown would ever have got elected at all) we shall never know, but it is a reasonable bet that it would have been a colourful administration. George Brown was one of the most interesting and well-loved political figures of the 1960s. He was born into politics, being roped in to help with canvassing from the age of eight. He left school at fifteen and trained for a career in trade unionism before becoming MP for Belper in 1945. He was an able, if very emotional, politician, and was not infrequently found to be as emotional as a newt. The expression 'tired and emotional' was actually first coined to describe his lapses from sobriety and was used as the title of his biography. He became Deputy Leader of the Labour party in 1960. In the first Wilson government he served as Secretary of State for Economic Affairs at the newly formed Ministry of the same name, a post which put him on a more or less permanent collision course with the Treasury. From 1966 to 1968 he was Foreign Secretary.

One of his most celebrated lapses came on the occasion of President Kennedy's assassination, when Brown was called unexpectedly from an event at which the drinks were flowing freely to give some reactions to the news on television. He was clearly genuinely upset by the news and was forced to take further sustenance in the hospitality room of the television studio, before going on. As his biographer Peter Paterson put it: 'Once on the air, Brown's performance was deeply, excruciatingly embarrassing, a compound of maudlin sentimentality, name-dropping and aggression.'

He presented himself as an intimate friend of the Kennedys (he had met them three times since Kennedy was elected), waved his arms about uncontrollably and slurred his speech. He was taken aside afterwards by Labour leader Harold Wilson and made to apologise to the parliamentary Labour party for his behaviour. This apology was then leaked to the press, something for which he blamed Wilson, further fuelling the bad feeling between them. Brown was not a man to hide his feelings towards people. When Len Williams was made Governor-General of Mauritius in 1968, Brown asked him whether his duties would require him to wear a plumed hat. When told that it would, Brown told him: 'Well, I hope your f**king feathers all fall out.'

On another occasion, his less-than-sober romantic overtures at a diplomatic function were rebuffed in the following memorable terms: 'I shall not dance with you for three reasons. First, because you are drunk. Second, because this is not a waltz but the Peruvian national anthem. And third, because I am not a beautiful lady in red; I am the Cardinal Bishop of Lima.'

Brown resigned from the Foreign Office in March 1968 after accusing Wilson of running a 'dictatorial administration'. After a spell on the back benches, the House of Commons was deprived of his services entirely in 1970, when he lost his seat in the general election and became the Life Peer Lord George-Brown. In 1982, three years before his death, he left his wife of forty years to go and live in a cottage in Cornwall with a former secretary forty years his junior.

He was an able, if very emotional, politician, and was not infrequently found to be as emotional as a newt

CHAPTER 7

THE PROFUMO AFFAIR

The increasing horror of my situation did not become apparent to me for some time . . . Every witness who does not give the answer the police want is tampered with. Every person who goes abroad has fled. Every person who speaks for me does so from fear. Every motive I had is twisted. . . . God alone knows what will happen.

Stephen Ward

CHRISTINE WHO?

A government caught up in 'the London underworld of vice, dope, marijuana, blackmail, counter-blackmail, violence and petty crime'

The Profumo scandal very nearly bought down the Conservative government and effectively marked the end of Harold Macmillan's time as Prime Minister. It enabled opposition leader Harold Wilson to speak in the Commons of a government caught up in 'the London underworld of vice, dope, marijuana, blackmail, counter-blackmail, violence and petty crime. . . . After the Vassall case [the Prime Minister] felt that he could not stand another serious case involving a ministerial resignation, and he gambled desperately and hoped that nothing would come out. For political reasons, he was gambling with national security.'

It all started quietly enough. On 15 March 1963 *The Times* ran what looked like a non-story. Rumours had been circulating that the Secretary of State for War, John Profumo, had offered to resign for unspecified personal reasons, but had been persuaded by Prime Minister Harold Macmillan to stay on. Reporters buttonholed Profumo on his way home and asked if there was any reason why he should resign. 'None whatsoever,' he replied.

The story appeared to end there, for John Profumo was a man who seemed to have it all. Descended from Italian aristocracy, he had enjoyed a privileged upbringing (Harrow and Oxford) and had been elected to Parliament in 1940 aged twenty-five, the youngest MP in the House. He had served in a number of ministerial positions and in some quarters there was talk of him as a possible future Prime Minister. Additional glamour attached to him through his marriage to the former film star Valerie Hobson, whose starring credits prophetically included *Great Expectations*,

The Spy in Black and *The Bride of Frankenstein*. However, some thought Profumo had rather too much of a liking for certain of life's pleasures and one of his party colleagues described him as: 'Not a man ever likely to tell the absolute truth in a tight corner.' Significantly, George Wigg, an influential Labour MP and confidant of Harold Wilson, had formed the same view of Profumo in his previous dealings with the Minister. Profumo certainly enjoyed the trappings of his position and his social life was spent in the company of the great and the good. His circle of friends included Lord Astor, whose monumental Thames-side family home, Cliveden, was to be the setting for the start of the whole affair.

In the same edition of *The Times* that carried the resignation non-story, just two columns away they ran a seemingly unrelated story about a trial at the High Court. A West Indian salesman called John Edgecombe was charged with shooting at his former girlfriend with intent to kill her. Edgecombe admitted firing the shots, but said it was done purely to frighten her – he had no intention of murder. The

Harold Wilson used the Profumo affair to link the government with sleazy elements of the criminal world.

trial became particularly newsworthy because the key witness – the ex-girlfriend – had gone missing, just when she was supposed to give evidence. The events in question had taken place at a flat where the girl's friend was staying. The friend's name was Marilyn Davies (better known later as Mandy Rice-Davies) and the missing girl was a twenty-year-old, described as a 'freelance model'. Her name was Christine Keeler. The flat concerned belonged to a society osteopath, Dr Stephen Ward.

There was enough evidence without Keeler's to send Edgecombe down for seven years. Labour MPs then began to ask why no attempt was being made to find a missing person who had so recently been the subject of an attempted shooting. But other, even more serious, stories were beginning to circulate. *Queen* magazine (Associate Editor Robin Douglas-Home, nephew of the then Foreign Secretary) ran a piece entitled 'Sentences I'd like to hear the end of', which was designed to pass on society gossip without running the risk of libel. It included the following, tantalisingly incomplete, sentence: 'Called in MI5 because every time the chauffeur-

Barbara Castle, one of the first MPs to blow the whistle on Profumo.

driven Zis drew up at her front door, out of the back door into a chauffeur-driven Humber slipped . . .'

On 22 March George Wigg used parliamentary privilege to make public rumours circulating in the House that Profumo was involved in Keeler's disappearance and in a possible perversion of the course of justice. Two other Labour MPs, Barbara Castle and Richard Crossman, were also involved in making the allegations. Next day – after a hurried meeting with senior members of the Conservative party – Profumo made a personal statement to the House of Commons. Watched from the public gallery by his wife and flanked by the Prime Minister, he said:

I last saw Christine Keeler in December 1961 and I have not seen her since. I have no idea where she is now. Any suggestion that I was in any way connected with or responsible for her absence from the trial at the Old Bailey is wholly and completely untrue.

My wife and I first met Miss Keeler at a house party in July 1961 at Cliveden. Among a number of people there was a Doctor Stephen Ward, whom we knew slightly, and a Mr Ivanov, who was an attaché at the Russian Embassy. Between July and December 1961 I met Miss Keeler on about half a dozen occasions at Doctor Ward's flat, when I called to see him and his friends. Miss Keeler and I were on friendly terms. There was no impropriety whatsoever in my acquaintanceship with Miss Keeler.

I have made this personal statement because of what was said in the House last evening by the three members and which was, of course, protected by privilege. I shall not hesitate to issue writs for libel and slander if scandalous allegations are made or repeated outside of the House.

In fact Profumo had been besotted with Christine Keeler since that first meeting. It had been a scorching hot June night and Keeler, staying with Ward in his cottage on the Cliveden estate, had gone up to the great house to swim in the pool. Egged on by Ward, she had dispensed with her swimming costume. Profumo was dining with Lord Astor and the two of them came out on to the terrace in their dinner-jackets, to find Keeler decidedly not dressed for dinner. Ward threw her costume behind a bush and Keeler was left to play chase with Astor and Profumo, to find something with which to cover herself. Just as the other dinner guests arrived on the terrace, Ward switched on the floodlights and Keeler found

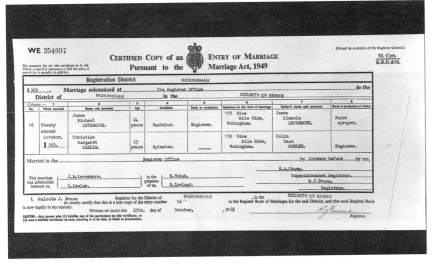

Christine Keeler was at the heart of the Profumo scandal. She later – briefly – became an honest woman (though her marriage certificate was strangely silent as to her profession).

herself being introduced to the distinguished group of dinner guests – including Profumo's wife – covered by a distinctly under-sized towel. Later that evening Profumo showed Keeler around the house. The conducted tour turned into another game of chase, this time through the bedrooms. And this time, Profumo won.

Profumo pursued the liaison with much more enthusiasm than Keeler. As she recalled, contrasting the social life she enjoyed in the company of other admirers: 'Jack never took me anywhere, except for drives all over London, and even then he was so anxious to be discreet that he used to borrow a big black car from Mr John Hare, the Minister of Labour.' Even their time together in Ward's flat was fraught with danger. Keeler again: 'There was that amazing evening when Jack was round, and an army colonel showed up suddenly, looking for Stephen. I had to introduce him to the War Minister. The colonel could not believe it. Jack nearly died.'

'HE WOULD DO, WOULDN'T HE?'

Despite the fact that Profumo's statement to the Commons raised as many questions as it answered, *The Times* took the view that this was an end to the matter. The only regret in their editorial was that Profumo had waited so long before clearing the air. Keeler turned up a few days later in Madrid, without any real explanation for her absence.

But things began to unravel for Profumo in April as first *Paris Match* and then the Italian magazine *Tempo Illustrato* ran stories about his relationship with Keeler. Profumo duly issued writs against them both, and *Tempo Illustrato* backed down. The government had supported Profumo as he made his personal statement, but at least some MPs had known for a long time that what he was saying was untrue. The Cabinet Secretary, Sir Norman Brook, had been tipped off by MI5 about the affair in 1961 and had warned Profumo against it, but he had continued seeing Keeler for months afterwards. Also in the picture at an early stage were the Soviet intelligence services at Moscow Central (thoroughly briefed by Kim Philby, according to one Russian source). In the meantime, Stephen Ward, mentioned in Profumo's statement, was being subjected to some very close investigation by the police, over allegations that he was living off immoral earnings. Ward said that it was in an effort to clear his own name that he wrote to the Home Secretary, alleging that certain aspects of Profumo's statement to the Commons were untrue.

These allegations were put to Profumo, who stuck to his story and was again believed. But by early June Profumo realised that his position had become untenable. Keeler was involved with some extremely unpleasant drug dealers and was talking to a lot of people about her relationship with 'somebody powerful', partly in an effort to warn off potential assailants. She had already been beaten up once in the street. She was also trying to sell her story to the *Sunday Pictorial*. Ward managed to persuade them not to print it, and it was a falling-out between Keeler and Ward over this that led to her falsely accusing Ward of living off immoral earnings.

Profumo told the Chief Whip of his decision to resign and wrote to the Prime Minister, saying that he had lied 'to protect, as I thought, my wife and family who were equally misled, as were my professional advisers'. His resignation was accepted without delay. Macmillan had himself for years been an unhappy victim of the adultery between his wife and parliamentary colleague Bob Boothby. Moreover, Profumo's crime had not just been a sexual peccadillo. At the same time as Profumo was seeing Christine Keeler, she was also entertaining the Russian, Mr Ivanov, mentioned in Profumo's personal statement. Yevgeny Ivanov was officially a Soviet Naval Attaché at their London Embassy, but was in reality a member of Soviet Military Intelligence. Ivanov recalls meeting Christine Keeler in his lurid memoirs. He described her as: 'A semi-literate, naive provincial girl with loose morals. . . . Christine was a dangerous creature, sly and treacherous. Her eyes told me that; they shone with passion, sensuality and cunning.' (He, of course – a drunken adulterer and spy – was a model of probity.) According to his version: 'I allowed Christine to seduce me. That devil of a girl could seduce anybody!'

A semi-literate, naive provincial girl with loose morals

Cliveden, the monumental stately home at the centre of the scandal, and the notorious swimming pool where Profumo first met Christine Keeler.

I don't suppose he enjoyed it at all – a case of close your eyes and think of Mother Russia, no doubt. There were stories at the time that Ivanov had asked Keeler to find out about the timing of delivery of missile warheads to Germany, something which Keeler denied at the time, as did Ivanov in his memoirs some years later. Whether it was true or not, the thought of the Secretary of State for War and a Russian agent sharing the same mistress did not inspire confidence among Britain's military allies.

The Conservative party was in deep disarray about the affair. Enoch Powell was openly considering resignation over the way in which it had been handled and several other ministers were known to be extremely uncomfortable about it – not least because of the speculation about wider government involvement in the scandal. The Prime Minister himself was suddenly seen to be vulnerable – within four months he was to take early retirement on health grounds. (The extent of his ill-health may be judged from the fact that he lived another twenty-three years of extremely active life.)

Britain's reputation abroad also suffered. Some Americans wanted President Kennedy to postpone a planned visit to Britain, lest he became in some way tainted with the scandal (of which more, later). Coming as it did soon after the Vassall spy case and the salacious Duchess of Argyll divorce case, as *The Times* put it, 'Britain today is portrayed as a mixture of life at the French court before the Revolution, Hollywood in its worst days and like a Latin American country known for its political cynicism.' *Newsweek* ran a piece entitled 'The New Pornocracy' which spoke of Britain's sex and spying scandal being 'a sort of World Parliament of prostitutes, whore-mongers, sex-deviates, orgy-prone highbinders, and libidinous Soviet agents'.

The image of Swinging London may be based in no small part on these events.

A sort of World Parliament of prostitutes, whore-mongers, sex-deviates, orgy-prone highbinders, and libidinous Soviet agents

A VICTIM IS FOUND

The real victim of the affair was Stephen Ward. He had set up business in London as an osteopath in 1946. Within a few years he had an appointment book which looked, in his own words, 'like the invitation lists to film premieres'. His patients included Frank Sinatra, Elizabeth Taylor, multi-millionaire Paul Getty, King Peter of Yugoslavia, Winston Churchill and Mahatma Gandhi. (Churchill, on hearing that Ward had treated Gandhi for a stiff neck, complained 'It was a pity you did not twist it right off'.) Ward was also a talented artist, who had an exhibition running in central London even as he went on trial. No fewer than eight members of the royal family had sat for him, as had leading politicians from the Prime Minister down. Ward had long moved in an elite and highly decadent circle, whose staple entertainment was a cocktail of sex, drugs and, well, more sex (rock and roll not yet having been invented in the early 1950s). An account of one of their little soirées seemed to involve eating such delicacies as roast peacock and stuffed badger to the sound of a rubber-masked masochist being whipped, while your hostess entertained half a dozen male guests on a nearby bed. (I know what you're thinking –

what is the point of going out for a meal when you can get all that sort of thing at home?) The domestic routine of at least one member of this group, nightclub owner Horace ('Hod') Dibben and his young bride (thirty-six years his junior) Mariella Novotny, made it to the Sunday newspapers. As Horace told the panting press: 'She used to tie me to a chair in my leather suit, whip me and then make me watch while she screwed someone in front of me.' Sometimes Mariella would combine business with pleasure by providing similar services for other members of their circle, for money, with Hod's evident approval: 'I liked her to earn a few bob on the side. It made her feel independent.' (As if tying her husband up and whipping him would not purge her of any sense of dependency.) Within this wholesome circle, which also included such people as the slum landlord Peter Rachman and insurance swindler Emil Savundra, as well as many more mainstream celebrities and men of influence, Ward became known as 'the provider of popsies for rich people'.

Ward was fascinated by women and cast himself in the role of Professor Higgins. He ran an early and radical version of the Youth Opportunities Programme, in which he would take young girls and educate them in the social graces (plus one or two other skills that your aunty might not necessarily regard as social graces) until they were able to move comfortably in his elite circles. Two of these trainees were Christine Keeler and Mandy Rice-Davies. Keeler was the product of a broken home, and she had been brought up in a converted railway carriage near Staines with her mother and stepfather. She came to London to be a showgirl, met Stephen Ward and, after two dates, moved in with him. She was later to be the mistress of Peter Rachman, enjoying some of his more select accommodation along with his unsavoury attentions.

Whether or not Ward received money for his 'introductions' is doubtful. It appeared that many of his protégées owed him far more money than they ever gave him. What is clear is that his subsequent trial was a mockery of justice. The Establishment closed ranks around Profumo and the government, while Ward was made a scapegoat and all those he had thought of as his friends deserted him. Most cases of living off immoral earnings were dealt with in the Magistrates' Courts and were punished with fines or probation. Ward's case was deemed to merit an eight-day trial at the Old Bailey, and he was prosecuted by Mervyn Griffith-Jones (the prosecuting counsel in the *Lady Chatterley* case, once described as a man who could make a honeymoon sound sordid).

The police had conducted an obsessive search for evidence of a crime (any crime – MI5 told the Commissioner of the Metropolitan Police to find *something* to pin on Ward, to shut him up). In what should have been a minor investigation, the police interviewed no fewer than 140 people. Some were interviewed repeatedly (Keeler was seen at least thirty-eight times). Mandy Rice-Davies was harassed by the police into testifying – they confiscated her passport, kept her imprisoned for ten days and lodged trumped-up charges of theft against her, which were later withdrawn. According to Davies herself,

Mervyn Griffith-Jones (the prosecuting counsel in the Lady Chatterley *case, once described as a man who could make a honeymoon sound sordid)*

at the end of her spell of imprisonment the officers running the case had said to her: 'Mandy, you don't like it here very much, do you? So help us and we'll help you.'

Another of the witnesses for the prosecution, Ronna Ricardo (or, as she was known professionally, Ronna the Lash), was subjected to intense pressure during her nine interviews. It subsequently emerged that she gave false evidence after the police threatened to have her child taken into care. Another witness also confessed to lying, then mysteriously withdrew her confession. Christine Keeler's evidence was allowed to stand against Ward, despite the fact that, even as the Ward trial was going on, Keeler was being found guilty of perjury in another case elsewhere in the same courts.

The trial became a national entertainment, giving rise to a host of flagellation jokes and infinite speculation about who else might be involved. There were rumours that the new American President, John F. Kennedy, had enjoyed the favours of another of Ward's girls during a party hosted by singer Vic Damone. The *Daily Mirror* even went to the trouble of denying Prince Philip's involvement, pretty well before anyone had even suggested it, though HRH had known Ward socially since the 1940s and had more recently sat for one of his drawings. By the end of the trial, it was said that: 'The scandal had now reached the point at which almost anything could be said about anyone; provided it was sufficiently scabrous, it was certain of wide circulation.'

Right to the end Ward was convinced that some of his powerful friends would rescue him. He was a man of fragile ego, with some previous history of attempted suicide. But by the end of the trial it became clear that the cavalry was not about to appear over the horizon. As the judge added his contribution to the shameful proceedings by strongly leading the jury to convict, Ward took an overdose of nembutal, from which he died before he could be sentenced. His last words, in his suicide note, were: 'It was surprisingly easy and required no guts. I am sorry to disappoint the vultures. I only hope this has done the job. Delay resuscitation as long as possible.'

The whitewash did not end there. The Master of the Rolls, Lord Denning, was brought in to investigate the security aspects of the affair, as well as providing – as Macmillan later put it – at least some check in the flood of accusation and rumour. His report, which was published in the autumn of 1963, earned the unique distinction for an HMSO publication of going on sale at midnight to satisfy the queue of eager purchasers outside the shops. It concluded that there had been no breach of security, and went out of its way to be polite about Profumo, while vilifying Ward as 'utterly immoral' and 'a man of vicious sexual activities'. Denning later went so far as to describe Ward as 'the most evil man I have ever met'. This, coming from a man whose profession brought him into daily contact with some of the nation's most spectacular criminals, shows a terrifying lack of perspective.

Lord Denning's state of mind may further be judged from his reported reaction to a photograph of Christine Keeler in a swimming costume. From looking at this, his forensic training evidently told him, 'you could readily infer her calling'. (What would he have made of a picture of the

I am sorry to disappoint the vultures. I only hope this has done the job. Delay resuscitation as long as possible.

England ladies' swimming team?) His report was even written like a second-rate Victorian detective novel, with melodramatic sub-headings like 'Christine tells her story', 'The lawyers are called in' and 'Mr Profumo's disarming answer'.

Ludovic Kennedy described the Denning report as a disgrace. Lord Denning produced all sorts of dirt, with no evidence. Parts of the evidence were allegedly so shocking to Denning's ears that he sent the stenographers out and no written record of it was kept. Witnesses said that he questioned them closely on the most sordid and irrelevant aspects of the case. Even Denning himself admitted to 'unavoidable limitations' in his report and apparently tried later to have the papers relating to it destroyed. One serving MI5 officer at that time claimed that Denning would certainly have had the wool pulled over his eyes, and would have been shown doctored files. It was a shameful episode in the career of a man normally held up as one of the century's greatest jurists.

The whole matter was debated in the House of Commons, and would-be spectators queued for three days to get a ringside seat. Labour had to argue that they were only interested in the security aspects of the case, though in reality they wanted to use the moral arguments to point to the decline of the government and to call for Macmillan's resignation. The Conservatives, for their part, had to try and stick to the moral arguments of the case, since these were the only ones on which Macmillan was relatively blameless. The debate was perhaps most memorable for the put-down of Lord Hailsham by one of Profumo's remaining supporters, Reginald Paget. Hailsham had made it his business to go around the country, railing against Profumo's sins but, as Paget put it, Hailsham's performance was: 'A virtuoso performance in the art of kicking a friend in the guts.' Hailsham, Paget said, was one of those who 'compound for sins they are inclined to commit by damning those they have no mind to . . . When self-indulgence has reduced a man to the shape of Lord Hailsham, sexual continence involves no more than a sense of the ridiculous.' At the end of the debate, the House moved on from the joyful contemplation of Lord Hailsham in flagrante delicto to the setting of standards for non-alcoholic drinks.

This was probably the last time the British public felt it necessary to strike a puritanical posture in relation to a sexual scandal of this kind. In fact, while maintaining an outward appearance of outrage, the public enjoyed it enormously.

A virtuoso performance in the art of kicking a friend in the guts

CONSPIRACY

Conspiracy theorists have had a rewarding time with the Ward/Profumo case over the years. One theory was that Profumo stumbled into an MI5 'honeypot' operation, the aim of which was to get the Soviet official Ivanov to defect, using the services of Ward and his protégées. Ivanov was in Britain for the purpose of espionage, in particular in relation to submarine and radar projects at the Portland naval base, and was highly connected within the Soviet power structure. His father-in-law was the

Chairman of the Supreme Court of the USSR. Lord Astor may well have been instrumental in introducing Ward to MI5, having formerly been in naval intelligence himself. Ward had also acted as a channel of communication between the Russian and British governments during the Cuban missile crisis, getting messages from Ivanov's contacts in Russia through to the Prime Minister himself.

Profumo left public life and devoted his remaining years to charitable works (for which he was awarded the CBE in 1975). He remained married to Valerie Hobson and seriously rich. Christine Keeler lives much more modestly off the proceeds of her memoirs. Yevgeny Ivanov was recalled to Moscow well before the scandal broke and retired to a flat in Moscow. Lord Denning remained Master of the Rolls until 1982 and enjoyed a longevity which was remarkable even for a judge, dying in 1999 aged 100. George Wigg, who first questioned Profumo's morals in Parliament, was made a life peer and Chairman of the Horse Race Betting Levy Board in 1967. He was later found guilty of kerb-crawling in Soho and died in 1983.

One 1960s innovation that didn't catch on – the Initial Teaching Alphabet.

The view most of us had of the moon landing.

CHRONICLE OF THE 1960s: SCIENCE AND TECHNOLOGY

14 March 1960: Plans for Thames Flood Barrier announced.

July 1960: The first laser demonstrated at Hughes Research, Malibu, California. (It stands for Light Amplification by Stimulated Emission of Radiation, so it is really a labseor.)

Also in 1960: The first fibre-tipped pen, from Pentel; the first all-transistor television from Sony; the first meteorological satellite, Tiros I; vaccines for measles and rubella; the oral contraceptive; the first vertical take-off jet fighter, the Hawker Siddeley P1127.

23 July 1962: First transmission of transatlantic television pictures via the satellite Telstar. Joe Meek records a single of the same name with the Tornadoes, which gets to number one for five weeks.

7 March 1967: First North Sea gas comes ashore at Easington, County Durham.

3 May 1968: Britain's first heart transplant.

21 July 1969: First men set foot on the moon. While they are there, Russia lands an unmanned spacecraft about 500 miles away from them, but nobody notices.

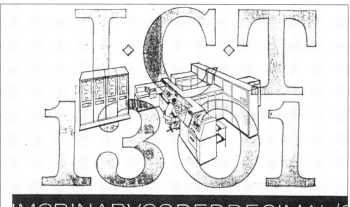

I·C·T 1301

IMCBINARYCODEDDECIMAL/S
TERLINGUPTO8DRUMSEACHOF

A computer is so much more than its specification

It is the sum of the thinking, the engineering, the experience that goes into its making, plus the accumulated skills that go into its applications and servicing. On all these scores, I·C·T have no equal in Britain. I·C·T, with over 50 years' experience of data processing, have made more than half the computers in commercial use here today. I·C·T in Britain is deployed over 23 factories, 31 area offices, 3 research establishments and 5 educational and training centres for customers' and I·C·T staff. World-wide, I·C·T employs 19,000 people and operates in 51 countries. I·C·T's service is at your service from the moment of your first enquiry. A comprehensive booklet on I·C·T's 1301 Computer can be had from the address below.

SOME DETAILS OF THE 1301

Fully transistorised
Central processor operates at 1 megacycle
Up to 8 drums each storing 12,000 words (144,000 digits)
Up to 24,000 digits of core storage
Magnetic tapes at 10 k/c or 22·6 k/c
Card input and line printing 600 per minute
Card output 100 per minute

International Computers and Tabulators Limited ICT 349 PARK LANE, LONDON, W1 · TELEPHONE: HYDE PARK 8080

£60,000,000 backs the certainty of the Century

Backed by a £60 million investment in research, engineering, software, training and new manufacturing plant, the NCR Century series is the world's most advanced new family of computers. NCR's long experience in designing business systems and all their knowledge of electronic data processing now combine with a range of new technological developments to give the Century series a cost/performance ratio unequalled in the computer field.
The Century series is now being produced by NCR to meet the hundreds of orders already received. Its unique features, built in with the help of new automatic manufacturing processes, will change the ideas of every business about computer capabilities and costs. All the resources of NCR including 80,000 employees back the certainty of the Century. Find out how this new computer family can meet *your* data processing needs efficiently, economically—and on time.

NCR sets the pace with the world's best computer buy

The advanced technological features of the Century include:
☐ Thin film short rod memories With 800 nanosecond cycle time and capacities from 16,384 to 524,288 characters.
☐ Monolithic integrated circuits throughout with high degree of standardisation to reduce manufacturing costs and simplify maintenance.
☐ New dual spindle disc unit with storage capacity of 8.4 million characters and transfer rate of 166,000 to 180,000 characters per second.
☐ Advanced software, including the easy-to-learn, easy-to-use NEAT/3.
☐ Common data in/16 support ... from three to nine-way simultaneity with multi-programming facilities.
☐ Complete upward compatibility in both hardware and software throughout the series.

Call in an NCR man for the story of the Century

See the Century presentation on Stand 56 at the Business Efficiency Exhibition

NCR

THE NATIONAL CASH REGISTER COMPANY LTD
206 Marylebone Road London NW1 Tel: 01-723 7070

'don't thank me – thank our Ferranti computer'

FERRANTI
RANGE OF COMPUTER SYSTEMS
PEGASUS · MERCURY · PERSEUS · ARGUS
SIRIUS · ORION · ATLAS

Computers arrive – and confuse us much more efficiently than the manual systems they replaced.

It was a rare school that had even one computer in the 1960s.

NEW COMPUTER

IMPORTANT new developments in the further use of computers for the payment of national insurance benefits are foreshadowed in the Ministry of Pensions and National Insurance annual report published this week.

A special chapter dealing with mechanisation says that next year the Ministry, which has for some time had two computer installations at Newcastle, handling graduated contribution records, pay and statistics, proposes to instal a computer at Reading for calculating and paying sickness, injury and unemployment benefits.

The days when the installation of a new computer was newsworthy.

New technology, new careers – but now as outmoded as handloom weavers.

CHAPTER 8

FROM OLD STAGER TO YOUNG SHAVER: SPORTING HEROES

He knew exactly when, and where, to go. People could never tackle him, and nobody could touch him for speed over ten yards. Even when he was nearing fifty, he still had his magic.

Bobby Charlton on Stanley Matthews

I always thought I was better than anyone else. It was up to them to get the ball off me – and they couldn't.

George Best on himself

FOOTBALL HEROES

The big footballing story of the 1960s for the English was, of course, their 1966 World Cup win. But the story has passed into cliché and instead we will look at two footballers at opposite ends of their careers in the 1960s, whose contrasting lives are illustrative of the changes that were taking place in sport during the decade.

Stanley Matthews – chased but rarely caught

In 1961 Stoke City Football Club made what seemed one of their riskier signings. They paid £3,500 for a forward and offered him a salary of £50 a week plus £25 appearance fee, which was a lot for a struggling second division side. Strangest of all, the player they bought was forty-six years old. On the positive side, there were (and are) not many players with the reputation of Stanley Matthews. In the event, it proved to be the best money they ever spent. In one week their gates went from around 8,000 to 35,288. This made Matthews even more popular among his team-mates, since the players got £1 each for every thousand in the crowd over 12,000. When Stoke were drawn in the Cup against last season's beaten finalists, Blackburn Rovers, the police were obliged to put a limit of 50,000 on the ground capacity.

Matthews was born in Hanley, the son of professional boxer Jack Matthews, the 'Fighting Barber'. He began his career at Stoke, as a fifteen-year-old schoolboy international, signed professional terms for them at seventeen and was a fixture in the England team by the age of nineteen. He played for England fifty-four times, plus twenty-four wartime internationals. In a career that was to span thirty-three years, Matthews never had his name taken by the referee. When news began to spread in Stoke that he was planning to leave the club, thousands of workers spontaneously downed tools and went on to the streets to protest. He none the less signed for Blackpool for £11,500 in 1947. Now, in 1961, he was returning to end his career at the club where it had started.

At his age, one might have expected Matthews to be a nine days' wonder for Stoke but, two seasons later, he popped up in the last game of the season, scoring the goal that ensured their promotion to the first division. His final match for them was on 6 February 1965, at the age of fifty years and five days, when he created one of the goals in their 3–1 win over Fulham. He was by then the oldest player ever to appear in a football league match. In the 1965 New Year's Honours List England's finest ever footballer became the first player to be knighted for his services to the game.

George Best – rarely chaste and often courted

Emerging at the same time was another 1960s footballing icon, who looks unlikely to be knighted unless the Queen introduces new categories of honours for services to alcohol and the opposite sex. We have now come to accept football as part of show business but in the 1960s footballers were more likely to smell of embrocation than aftershave. But George Best, also known as the fifth Beatle, was given showbusiness status in a way that Stanley Matthews could only dream (or possibly have nightmares) about.

Just about the time Matthews was re-signing for Stoke, Matt Busby bought a scraggy-looking teenager over from Belfast for a trial. Within a day, the homesick fifteen-year-old was on the ferry back home, but he had already shown Manchester United enough of his extraordinary skills. Busby got him back (dispatched back to Manchester, it was said, with the toe end of his father's boot) and this time the club persuaded him to stay. By the age of seventeen he had made the first team. After just fifteen first team appearances with United, he was selected to play for his country. (Best's father almost influenced his son's football career in a very different way. He was a strong believer in faith healing and, when Best injured a cartilage early on in his career, it took all Busby's powers of persuasion to get his player taken to a doctor, rather than a church. Surgery saved Best's

In the 1960s footballers were more likely to smell of embrocation than aftershave

*All-in wrestling – one of the
sporting feasts of the 1960s.*

career and he went on to be British and European Footballer of the Year in Manchester United's golden year, 1968.)

Best first made his name on the European scene in United's match against Benfica in the 1966 European Cup quarter-finals. Benfica were then the strongest side in Europe. They made up the majority of the Portuguese World Cup side and their star player Eusebio was given the award of European Footballer of the Year immediately before the match. United had travelled to Portugal with a slender one-goal lead from the first leg, and the last time they had played in that country they had been trounced 5–0. In the pre-match team talk Busby told the players to try to contain Benfica for the first quarter, before looking for opportunities to attack. Best hit upon the novel idea of containing them by scoring two goals in the first twelve minutes. By this time the crowd were entranced, and shouted 'El Beatle!' every time he got the ball. He went on to make another of the goals in their 5–1 victory.

However, it was not until 1968 that United and Best were to win the European Cup. This time, Benfica were their opponents in the final. Full time arrived with the match tied at 1–1. Eusebio managed to hit the goalkeeper instead of the gaping net in just about the last minute. As the exhausted players rested before extra time, Matt Busby demonstrated his total mastery of tactics. He told them: 'If you pass the ball to each other, you will beat them.' So that was it! Passing the ball to the other side was standing between them and victory! Inspired, the United team leapt up. Best danced past two of the opposition to put United in front, and they ran out easy 4–1 winners. Their European Cup victory helped to ease Matt Busby's self-imposed burden of guilt. He had made the decision to take the team into Europe – a decision that had brought them to disaster on a snowy runway in Munich.

Best had been frightened of Busby at first. He used to hide behind the bus queue if he saw the great man driving past, in case he offered him a lift. But after the European Cup victory, Best saw that the United team was ageing and stale. Busby had only bought one new player – goalkeeper Alex Stepney – in the last four years. Best bravely confronted Busby in his office, demanding that the likes of Bobby Charlton and Dennis Law should go, and that he should be made captain. His demands were refused and, although he stayed with United until the beginning of 1974, his relationship with the club went steadily downhill. There were repeated absences from Old Trafford and he was at one point put on the transfer list. For some strange reason, he began to find drinking champagne in the company of adoring women a more attractive proposition than running up and down a muddy field.

As the first of the modern footballing superstars, he made a good living from product endorsements. His name was used to sell hairspray, cosmetics and football boots, and one entrepreneur paid £25,000 for the use of his name on a range of clothes for the 5–13 age group. Best even had a chain of boutiques and was forced to make regular visits to London to keep up with the fashion scene. However, celebrity had its disadvantages: his E-type Jaguar was a regular target for graffiti artists; he was at one point besieged inside a flat he was visiting by a mob of hysterical schoolchildren (though, given that this was in London, they may have been young Arsenal supporters trying to lynch him); and his fanmail also contained the odd death threat from the unhinged. All this was in addition to the fate suffered by all gifted players on the field, where he became the regular target for the less talented hard men among his opponents.

Best first announced his retirement just before his 26th birthday, though he made a series of comebacks with a variety of different clubs. But by the age of fifty, when Stanley Matthews retired from the game, George Best's footballing skills were a distant memory. His great footballing days had been with Manchester United, for whom he played almost 450 games and scored nearly 200 goals. But Best had another record, one which Sir Stanley never got near, and which is unlikely ever to be broken – he dated no fewer than four different Miss Worlds.

How good was he? The views of the Miss Worlds are not recorded for posterity. But on the football field Matt Busby, who played alongside some of the legends of British football and can be regarded as a fair judge of players, believed 'George Best is possibly the greatest player on the ball that I have ever seen. You can remember Matthews, Finney, Mannion and all the great players of that era, but I cannot think of one who took the ball so close to an opponent to beat him with it as Best does.'

Best rarely played golf with his fellow players. As one of them explained: 'It's understandable. He doesn't like parting with the ball.'

Best had another record, one which Sir Stanley never got near – he dated no fewer than four different Miss Worlds

MOTOR RACING IS DANGEROUS

In April 1968 Jim Clark interrupted his bid for a third Formula 1 motor racing championship to take part in a minor Formula 2 race at Hockenheim. He should not even have been at the race – but for a snag in registering his entry, he would have been at the BOAC 500 Race at Brands Hatch, trying out a new 200mph Ford prototype.

Clark was the greatest racing driver of his generation – one of the new breed of professionals. His career had started modestly enough in 1956, as a twenty-year-old racing a DKW saloon on a converted airfield near Aberdeen. Clark's first taste of single-seater driving only came in 1959 in Formula Junior, the forerunner to Formula Ford, but by 1960 his success was enough to win him a place in the proposed new Aston Martin Grand

In some forms of motor racing, the greatest risk was dying of embarrassment.

Prix team. Sadly, that project never came to fruition and he went off to drive Formula 2 cars for Lotus instead. During that season, he not only tied for the Formula 2 championship, but also got to drive for their Formula 1 team and took an Aston Martin DBR1 to third place in the Le Mans 24 hour race. Colin Chapman, the Lotus team manager, recognised the potential of his new signing. For the 1961 season, he sacked Innes Ireland, who had just won the American Grand Prix for Lotus, to give Clark a permanent place in the Formula 1 team.

The season bought Clark his first Grand Prix win, at Pau. It also involved him in one of motor racing's worst disasters. In September of that year the Italian Grand Prix at Monza saw the German Wolfgang Von Trips start in pole position in his Ferrari 156. Clark was some way behind him, but Von Trips made a slow start and towards the end of the first lap Clark was in his slipstream on the fast banked track. Clark pulled out to overtake but, just at the same moment, Von Trips moved in the same direction. Their wheels touched and the Ferrari shot up the banking, hitting a fence where spectators were packed, before rolling back down the track. Fourteen spectators were killed, and Von Trips was hurled from his car and perished with them. Clark escaped unhurt, and was found wandering about at the side of the track, dazed and in shock. It says much for his strength of character that he recovered sufficiently to come seventh in the American Grand Prix later that same season.

In 1963 Clark took his first World Championship, winning seven Grands Prix. He also drove a Lotus in American races for the first time. The Americans laughed at the funny little car, with its engine at the wrong end, but were forced to reconsider when the Lotus came second in the Indianapolis 500 and won the Milwaukee 200 later in the season.

Clark's second World Championship came in 1965, when he sewed up the championship by August. In 1967 Denny Hulme won the Championship, but Clark was the driver everybody was interested in. He won the United States Grand Prix with his rear suspension broken, the wheel hanging off the car at a crazy angle – but his speed only slightly reduced. Clark by now had one of the legendary combinations of motor racing history – the Lotus 49, powered by the Cosworth V8 engine.

The Italian Grand Prix of 1967 was held to be one of the classic drives in the history of Grand Prix racing. Clark led from the start, but a pitstop for tyre problems meant

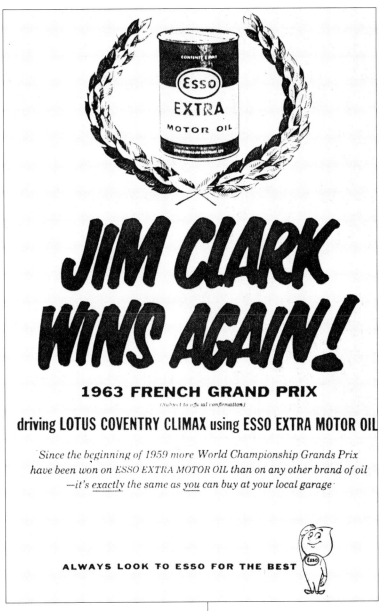

JIM CLARK WINS AGAIN!

1963 FRENCH GRAND PRIX
(Subject to official confirmation)

driving **LOTUS COVENTRY CLIMAX** using **ESSO EXTRA MOTOR OIL**

Since the beginning of 1959 more World Championship Grands Prix have been won on ESSO EXTRA MOTOR OIL than on any other brand of oil —it's exactly the same as you can buy at your local garage

ALWAYS LOOK TO ESSO FOR THE BEST

that he rejoined the race in 15th place, a full lap behind the leaders. Virtually nobody had ever made up such a deficit but, by lap 59, Clark's inspired driving had taken him to second place, with only his team-mate Graham Hill in front of him. Hill eventually had to retire, leaving Clark in the lead. He was closely pursued round the high-speed corners of Monza – the scene of his earlier disaster – by Brabham and Surtees. On the very last lap, as they were slipstreaming each other at 260kph, Clark's car started running out of petrol. After some hair-raising overtaking manoeuvres, Clark was forced to freewheel home in third place, in a race which he had morally won.

Everybody expected 1968 to be his year. Clark confirmed this expectation by winning the season's first Grand Prix, in South Africa. This took him to a total of twenty-five wins, passing the record set by Juan-Manuel Fangio.

Then came Hockenheim and the fatal accident. For a long time nobody was quite sure what made Clark crash at Hockenheim. The wreckage

> **Motor racing is very dangerous indeed**
> In the days before either drivers or promoters thought too much about safety, motor racing took a terrible toll of its participants. No fewer than twenty-five drivers, of Grand Prix standard alone, died in motor racing accidents in the 1960s:
>
> 1960   Harry Blanchard, Chris Bristow, Harry Schell, Alan Stacey
> 1961   Guilio Cabianca, Peter Ryan, Wolfgang Von Trips
> 1962   Ricardo Rodriguez
> 1963   Oscar Galvez
> 1964   Carel de Beaufort, Tim Mayer
> 1966   Walter Hansgen, John Taylor
> 1967   Bob Anderson, Lorenzo Bandini, Giacomo Russo, Ian Raby
> 1968   Jim Clark, Ludovico Scarfiotti, Jo Schlesser, Mike Spence
> 1969   Lucien Bianchi, Paul Hawkins, Gerhard Mitter, Moises Solana.

yielded no evidence of mechanical failure and nobody was betting on driver error with someone of Clark's skill. Striking a bird at high speed was one explanation, but more recent research puts it down to a deflated rear tyre. Clark died of a broken neck and skull fractures on 4 April 1968, aged just thirty-two. A highly strung, shy man, he hated all the publicity that was increasingly part of a Grand Prix driver's life. Clark was also a widely gifted man, proficient at cricket, playing the violin, dancing, hockey, sprinting and water-skiing. He was a very bad passenger in a car but, placed behind the wheel, he became relaxed, confident and competitive, without being suicidally dangerous. Graham Hill described him as the ideal racing driver. Motor racing had claimed one of its all-time greats.

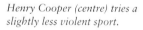

Henry Cooper (centre) tries a slightly less violent sport.

OUR 'ENRY

The 1960s marked the greatest years for the man who is arguably the most popular British boxer of recent years (though pantomime fans may wish to stake a claim for Frank 'Widow Twankey' Bruno's place in public affections). Londoner Henry Cooper won the British amateur light heavyweight championship as long ago as 1952, and turned professional on leaving the army two years later. He took first the British heavyweight title and then the European title from fellow Briton Brian London, in

1959 and 1964, but his finest hours came in his two fights with Cassius Clay.

Before the first fight at Wembley in 1963 Clay summed up the prospects with his usual disarming modesty. He declared that Cooper was 'a cripple and a bum' and that he would take him in five rounds. Few would have bet on this outcome at the end of the fourth round. In the last moments of that round, Cooper floored Clay with the punch known affectionately (except by those on the end of it) as ''Enry's 'Ammer'. Only the bell saved a clearly dazed Clay.

More to the point, Clay was saved by the discovery, during the interval, that one of his gloves had split. British fans have always been suspicious about this coincidence, since the changing of the gloves gave him time to recover his composure. In fact, so composed was Clay by the time that the bell went for the start of round five, that he came out and won the fight in that round, as predicted. Cooper was always vulnerable to cut eyes and these were once again to be his downfall.

For younger readers – this is what tennis racquets used to look like, before technology took over.

Cooper was given a proper world title fight against Clay (or Muhammed Ali, as he had become) in 1966. This was a great day for British boxing fans. The last Briton to hold the world heavyweight crown had been Cornishman Bob Fitzsimmons in 1897, and a Briton had not even fought for the title since 1908. Cooper entered the ring in a swirl of union jacks, with the hopes of the 45,000 crowd at Highbury football stadium resting on his shoulders. They had paid up to 20 guineas for a seat, and Cooper's share of the purse was to be £50,000. But few people gave him a serious chance against such an outstanding champion, who was also eight years his junior. Journalist Hugh McIlvanney described Cooper before the fight as 'the nicest fellow ever to be about to be defeated for the world heavyweight title'.

Cooper held his own for the first few rounds, and was thought by some to have won a couple of them, but his battle-scarred eyes let him down again. In the last couple of rounds Cooper's face was a horrific mess of blood as, half-blinded, he went for Ali, trying against all the odds to land the left hook that would win him the title. The referee put an end to his efforts after 1 minute 38 seconds of the sixth round. But Cooper went on to win three Lonsdale Belts in the defence of his British championship, before retiring in 1971.

In later years Cooper could lay claim to considerable credit for improving the grooming habits of the nation's manhood. His rugged countenance was chosen by the advertisers to demonstrate once and for all to a sceptical British public that after-shave was not effeminate. If 'Enry slapped it on, no one was going to argue with him – unless, of course, his name was Ali.

CHRONICLE OF THE 1960s:
SPORTING EVENTS

6 May 1961: Tottenham Hotspur become the first football team this century to achieve the FA Cup/League double.

8 July 1961: An all-English Ladies' Singles Final at Wimbledon produces the first British victor since Dorothy Round in 1937. Angela Mortimer wins in three sets after favourite Christine Truman falls.

23 April 1962: Stirling Moss is injured at Goodwood motor racing circuit.

July 1962: Last Gentlemen v. Players cricket match at Lords. For some reason, the MCC seem to think it is an anachronism. In the same month professional footballers win their campaign against the maximum wage.

17 March 1966: Arkle wins his third Cheltenham Gold Cup in a row.

27 March 1966: The stolen World Cup is found in a garden by a dog named Pickles.

30 July 1966: England win the World Cup. The feel-good factor disguises the £500 million austerity package brought in by the Labour government ten days earlier. The team even play in red shirts, as Alf Garnett explains, to make us think that it was the Labour government that won it for us.

6 June 1968: The first Wimbledon men's singles open to professionals is won by Rod Laver of Australia.

12 July 1969: Tony Jacklin becomes the first Briton to win the Open Golf Championship since 1951.

CHAPTER 9

FRIENDS AND NEIGHBOURS: IMMIGRATION AND RACE RELATIONS

Like the Roman, I see the River Tiber foaming with much blood.
Enoch Powell on the government's immigration policy, 20 April 1968

Britain has a long and disreputable track record of racism that is almost as old as the nation itself. Before the days of black settlement, those of a racist inclination had to content themselves with persecuting the Jews. The Magna Carta, that supposed beacon of freedom, contains anti-Jewish clauses and Edward I actually expelled the Jews from the country in the 1290 prototype of ethnic cleansing. They were not to return in any numbers until the seventeenth century, when Oliver Cromwell lifted the ban on their residence. Following a period of more intensive Jewish settlement in the late nineteenth century, the 1905 Aliens Act sought to prevent the entry of anyone who did not have the wherewithal to support themselves or the means to earn it. It also allowed the authorities to expel any new resident who tried to claim poor relief, became a vagrant or committed the heinous crime of living in overcrowded or insanitary conditions. The Act did at least establish the right of sanctuary for those found to be suffering from political or religious persecution.

Post-war labour shortages led immigrants from the new Commonwealth to come to Britain in large numbers, actively supported by the governments of the day (including a junior minister named Enoch Powell). The 1948 British Nationality Act gave Commonwealth citizens the right freely to enter the country, to work here and to settle with their families.

Post-war labour shortages led immigrants from the new Commonwealth to come to Britain in large numbers, actively supported by the governments of the day

LIFE AFTER NOTTING HILL

Race relations were uneasy at the start of the 1960s. The end of the previous decade had seen the race riots in Notting Hill and elsewhere. Full employment, which had meant that at least immigrants and the indigenous population were not competing to any great degree for jobs, was also starting to look a little less secure as the economy began to slow down. Active racial discrimination and the use of quite violently racist language was not controlled to any great degree at this time. People advertising jobs or letting property were free to specify 'No blacks'. Sir Gerald Nabarro, a Conservative MP not noted for the lightness of his touch or the moderation of his views (which was probably why he was in demand for broadcasting), appeared on the radio programme *Any Questions?* in 1963 and asked the audience: 'How would you feel if your

Racist views could be expressed much more openly in the 1960s, as this schoolgirl's questionnaire shows.

Sir Gerald Nabarro dispenses some more of his wisdom, but extremists outside the main parties made little impact at the polls.

daughter wanted to marry a big buck nigger with the prospect of coffee-coloured grandchildren?' When this created something of a stir, to put it mildly, the BBC decided to edit it out of the repeat of the programme 'in order to avoid perpetuating a misunderstanding'. For his part, Sir Gerald said that he had not meant to cause offence (which begs the appalling question of what the man would have said had he wished to cause offence. Here was someone who could teach Goebbels a thing or two about whipping up racist sentiment.) In similar vein senior Labour politician Patrick Gordon-Walker was ousted from his Smethwick constituency in 1964 by an overtly racist campaign that took as its slogan 'If you want a nigger neighbour, vote Labour'. Harold Wilson said that the successful candidate, local politician and headmaster Peter Griffiths, would serve his time in the House as a parliamentary leper. Labour won back Smethwick in 1966.

The story of race relations in the 1960s can be seen as two contrasting trends – one trying to control the level of immigration into the country, and the other moving towards a fairer society for those who were already here. The two strands of policy were felt to work in tandem with each other, in the belief that fewer immigrants would produce better race relations.

THE CHANGING LAW ON RACE AND IMMIGRATION

The first attempt to curb the rate of immigration was the 1962 Commonwealth Immigrants Act, which introduced a voucher system for anyone other than the dependants of those already here. A resolution at the Conservative party conference the previous October had called for the introduction of immigration controls. This, of course, encouraged those thinking about coming over to do so quickly, in order to beat the ban, which in turn added fuel to the fire for campaigners against the rising tide of immigration. Under the Act, vouchers would only be issued to those with (a) a specific job to come to; (b) a specific skill that was in short supply; or (c) a limited number of 'others' (with ex-servicemen getting some priority). Despite arguing against this while in opposition, the later Labour government in 1965 abolished category (c) and went on to introduce far stricter controls in 1968.

The 1965 Race Relations Act was the first attempt to establish equal rights for people of different races. It was seen in retrospect as being little more than window-dressing, since the criminal penalties originally envisaged for racist behaviour were watered down during the committee stage of the Bill to voluntary mechanisms to investigate allegations, and to offer conciliation when the two parties accepted it. It also omitted key areas such as housing and employment from its provisions. However, the greater importance of this piece of legislation was in shifting public opinion towards the idea that there needed to be such safeguards, and thus it laid the foundation for further legislation in the future.

From the early 1960s a number of the newly independent African former colonies pursued a policy of 'Africanisation', designed to squeeze out the large numbers of people of Asian origin who had settled there and had in many cases formed a successful business class. Indian Prime Minister Mrs Gandhi had privately offered to give them a home but could not say so publicly, since it was felt this would just make it easier for the governments concerned to proceed with their ethnic cleansing policies. Kenya started expelling Asians in a big way in the autumn of 1967. It was estimated that about 170,000 of their population were eligible to apply for British passports and that, by October of that year, about half of those had done so.

As they arrived, at a rate of up to 1,000 a week, the increasing influx led to the hurried passing of the 1968 Commonwealth Immigrants Act. The Act reduced the number of vouchers under the 1962 scheme and also introduced the idea of 'patriality'. This meant that in order to qualify for entry and residence in Britain you, or one of your parents or grandparents, had to be born, adopted or naturalised in the UK. A British passport no longer gave automatic right of residence here. The effect of this was to exclude many groups, such as the African Asians, while still leaving the door open to many of the white residents of Australia, Canada and even South Africa (which was no longer part of the Commonwealth). It meant, too, that there was a whole group of people who – regardless of their formal citizenship – were left stateless.

The 1968 Race Relations Act was again preceded by a big 'hearts and minds' offensive by the then Home Secretary, Roy Jenkins. A number of supportive articles appeared in the media before the Bill came to Parliament. For the first time talk of 'assimilation' (whereby the immigrant population becomes absorbed into the majority and loses its separate identity) was replaced by the idea of 'multi-

Malcolm X – race relations polemicist – offers a point of view at a public meeting.

Roy Jenkins, Home Secretary for many of the race relations reforms of the 1960s.

culturalism'. The Act clarified the role of the Race Relations Board, which until that time had been trying to combine the roles of promoter of good race relations and policeman against bad behaviour. It set up the Community Relations Council to do the promotional work and left the watchdog role to the Board. Equally important was its extension of the law against discrimination into areas such as housing, employment, the provision of goods, facilities or services, and the publication of notices and advertisements.

Housing was one of the major flashpoints for racial tension at the time. Many immigrants could only afford the worst inner city properties, for which building societies would not normally lend money. Unscrupulous lenders stepped in, offering short-term, high interest mortgages. The result was that immigrant landlords had to subdivide their properties to extreme degrees to keep up the repayments, or several immigrant families would have to collaborate to buy a single property, which they then occupied in grossly overcrowded conditions. Estate agents also got in on the act: those in Brixton, one of the main areas of settlement, were known to increase the prices of houses to immigrants, or to demand extra commission or payments 'under the table' to secure property.

ENOCH POWELL AND THE 'RIVERS OF BLOOD'

Enoch Powell was described at one time as the 'enfant terrible' of the Conservative party. An outstanding scholar, he became Professor of Greek at Sydney University at the age of just twenty-five and he was a monetarist in his economic thinking, long before Keith Joseph and Margaret Thatcher brought it to the heart of Conservative policy. From 1950 he was Member of Parliament for Wolverhampton, an area which received a considerable number of the post-war immigrants. His relationship with the mainstream Conservative party was always tempestuous. He resigned from the Treasury in 1958, threatened to do so again over the handling of the Profumo affair and refused to serve under Sir Alec Douglas-Home. He stood against Edward Heath for the party leadership in 1965, but came bottom of the poll, with only 13 votes to Heath's 150. His views on both the Common Market and immigration made him a controversial figure, both within the party and outside.

Never was he more controversial than on 20 April 1968 (the anniversary of Hitler's birthday, as it happened), when he spoke against the 1968 Race Relations Bill. He used the opportunity to call for a complete stop to immigration and the introduction of repatriation for those who were already here. The tone of his speech was uncompromising and some of it (though he never used quite the words the tabloid newspapers reported) sounded to those who wanted to hear it that way like an incitement to violence. He spoke of English people who

> found themselves made strangers in their own country. They found their wives unable to find hospital beds in childbirth, their children unable to find school places, their homes and neighbourhoods changed beyond recognition, their plans and prospects for the future defeated.

Enoch Powell was described at one time as the 'enfant terrible' of the Conservative party

[The Bill] is to be enacted to give the stranger, the disgruntled and the agent provocateur the power to pillory [Britons] for their private actions. Here is the means of showing that the immigrant community can organise to consolidate their members, to agitate and campaign against their fellow citizens, and to overawe and dominate the rest with the legal weapons which the ignorant and the ill-informed have provided. . . . We must be mad, literally mad, as a nation to be permitting the annual inflow of some fifty thousand dependants of immigrants. . . . it is like watching a nation busily engaging in heaping up its own funeral pyre. . . . As I look ahead I am filled with foreboding. Like the Roman, I see the River Tiber foaming with much blood.

KHAN'S

menu
ENGLISH AND INDIAN

PLAIN, MADRAS AND BIRIYANI CURRY DISHES A SPECIALITY

CHICKEN	Prices from
BEEF	3/- to 7/6
PRAWN	approx.
SCAMPI	Boiled or Plain
KEEMA	Rice Included
EGG	5/- Chips
Roast or Fried Chicken	included

All dishes supplied in foil containers.

70 LOWER HILLGATE STOCKPORT

TAKE OUT
ONLY

CURRY CENTRE

ORIENTAL FRUITS AND FOODS

OPENING
MONDAY, JUNE 16th
11-30 a.m. to 11 p.m.
7 DAYS PER WEEK INCLUDING HOLIDAYS

Asian food makes a tentative appearance on the British culinary scene.

He went on from this reference to classical literature to a rather more down-to-earth account of one of his elderly white female constituents, living in a largely black area, who had allegedly had excrement pushed through her letterbox.

Powell was not alone in his views among the Conservative leadership. Former Cabinet Minister Duncan Sandys had spoken in 1967 of 'the breeding of millions of half-caste children [that] would merely produce a generation of misfits and create racial tension'. Sandys' speech attracted no criticism from the Conservative party hierarchy, and he also survived an attempt to prosecute him under the existing race relations law. However, the reaction to Powell's speech was enormous. Edward Heath condemned it as racist and sacked him from the shadow cabinet, and many others were appalled by both the speech itself and the sensationalised 'rivers of blood' accounts of it in the tabloid press. But in the country at large Powell found a huge groundswell of support.

In one typical town – Reading – in the days that followed the speech, letters in the local press called for an immigration ban and repatriation; local Conservative parties passed pro-Powellite motions and Conservative members of Earley parish council quit the party in support of Powell, to form a local branch of the National Front. Building workers walked off their sites in support of his policies and an attempt by the Reading Trades Council to condemn their action led to a split in the council itself. Powell himself came to address the Reading University Conservative Association and only a huge police presence prevented the thousand or so demonstrators outside from wrecking the meeting (a similar gathering at Exeter in the same week had ended in a riot).

Enoch Powell's views on race relations cast him out of the mainstream of British politics.

The controversy put Powell outside the mainstream of British politics for the rest of his life. Reaction to the speech also helped Harold Wilson's somewhat flagging fortunes. Wilson responded to the speech by launching a new urban programme initiative in areas with large immigrant populations. Speaking a few days later at Birmingham Town Hall, as mounted police controlled restive crowds outside, Wilson said:

> I am not prepared to stand aside and see this country engulfed by the racial conflict which calculating orators or ignorant prejudice can create. Nor, in the great world confrontation on race and colour, where this country must declare where it stands, am I prepared to be a neutral. In these issues there can be no neutrals.

Support for Powell in the Conservative party itself was striking. The Conservative Political Centre carried out a confidential poll of 412 constituency groups in December 1968. They found that 327 of them wanted all immigration stopped indefinitely, and a further 55 wanted only strictly limited quotas of dependants allowed in and a five-year ban on further immigration. Some wanted special housing areas for immigrants to be set up, along the lines of South African apartheid, while one even wanted to set up permanent camps to house the immigrants. In the country as a whole, a Gallup poll in April 1968 showed Powell having a wide body of support. About 70 per cent of those surveyed thought there was some danger of race riots and a small majority (53 per cent) thought there should be no law against refusing to sell or let a house on racial grounds.

Powell himself claimed that he was not racist, that he did not despise anyone on the grounds of race or think them inferior. His argument was rather to do with them residing in – but not belonging to – Britain. In his view, future generations of black people would remain as outsiders to the mainstream of British society, no matter where they were born. Birth in the United Kingdom might make them a UK citizen, but it did not make

Trans-racial adoptions provoked strong reactions in the 1960s – just as they do today, although perhaps for different reasons.

Mixed-race marriage was also rare enough to be considered newsworthy in some areas.

them English – that, for him, was the product of common heritage and ancestry. His policy was therefore to call for an end to immigration and the establishment of a Ministry of Repatriation.

BLACKBALLED – THE 1968 MCC TOUR

For those of a racist persuasion, the apartheid South African regime stood like a bastion of good government. Others saw it as a pariah in world politics. The year 1968 brought an illustration of the extent to which sport and politics were irrevocably entwined in that country. There was an outcry among both cricket fans and those opposed to apartheid when Basil D'Oliveira was not initially selected for the MCC tour to South Africa that year. He had scored 158 in the final test against Australia that same season. The MCC selectors insisted that the choice had been made on ability alone, but anti-apartheid groups seized upon the fact that D'Olivera, who came from South Africa, was classified there as Coloured.

Members of the MCC attempted to organise protest meetings to challenge the selection and the Revd David Shepherd, himself a former

Immigrants are trained in their new language.

England cricket captain, wrote in the Church of England newspaper in favour of cancelling the tour. White feathers for cowardice were sent to the MCC for their failure to select D'Olivera. The then current England captain Colin Cowdrey attempted to defend the MCC, creating a hostage to fortune by saying that any attempt by the South African government to interfere with team selection would lead to the tour's cancellation.

In the midst of this, the *News of the World* recruited D'Olivera to cover the tour for them. This brought a new dimension to the dispute, since apartheid also extended to the press boxes at the cricket grounds, into which Coloureds were only admitted in menial positions. Reporting for the *News of the World* was not considered menial enough, except by journalists for the quality dailies, and the South African press saw this as deliberately provocative.

However, when Tom Cartwright, one of the chosen team, dropped out through injury, D'Olivera's selection for the tour party became unavoidable. Almost as inevitable was the reaction of South African Prime Minister P.W. Vorster, who described the touring party as: 'No longer a cricket team, but a team of trouble-makers for South Africa's separate development policies.' He made an outspoken attack on the whole business:

No longer a cricket team, but a team of trouble-makers for South Africa's separate development policies

> The team as constituted now is not the team of the MCC but the team of the Anti-Apartheid Movement, the team of the South African Non-Racial Olympic Committee and the team of Bishop Reeves.* We left it to the MCC to make their choice. We did not want to play selection committee for them. The ultimate decision was theirs and theirs only, and they made their choice on merit. There was an immediate outcry because a certain gentleman of Colour was omitted on merit, as they themselves said. From then on, D'Olivera was no longer a sportsman but a political cricket ball. From then on, it was political bodyline bowling all the way.

There was much criticism of his speech even at home, since South Africans were rapidly becoming the sporting lepers of the world. They were barred from the 1968 Olympics and isolation in many other areas of sport was on its way. They would have drawn some comfort from the fact that the British Isles Bowls Tour of South Africa was to go ahead as planned. A Johannesburg businessman announced plans to invite a team of Cavaliers – made up of as many of the MCC party as they could attract – to replace the missing touring team.

But the MCC team toured Pakistan and Ceylon instead during the winter of 1968/69, with D'Olivera as one of the party. He went on to play a total of forty-four tests for England and was awarded the OBE in 1969.

*The deported anti-apartheid Bishop of Johannesburg.

CHAPTER 10

FROM DISCORD TO CONCORDE: TRANSPORT IN THE 1960s

There is a great emotional upsurge every time we propose to close a service. A week afterwards, it has all died away. This time, it might take a little longer.

Dr Richard Beeching, at the launch of his report

OH, DOCTOR BEECHING!

The whole enterprise operated on a set of economic principles that appeared to have been dreamed up at a Mad Hatter's Tea Party

By the start of the 1960s the British railways were in an appalling mess. Allowed to expand without proper control in the nineteenth century, there was vastly more track mileage than could be commercially justified; investment plans announced in the 1950s went nowhere near compensating for years of neglect and the labour force was underpaid, overmanned and riddled with restrictive practices. The whole enterprise operated on a set of economic principles that appeared to have been dreamed up at a Mad Hatter's Tea Party.

To give a few examples: half of the entire rail system accounted for just 4 per cent of the passenger traffic and 5 per cent of the freight. This part of the network did not generate enough income even to pay for the upkeep of the track, let alone the operation of trains on it. At the other extreme, the top thirty-four stations (just under half of 1 per cent of the total) took some 26 per cent of the revenue. A third of the 18,500 coaches in service spent most of their year rusting in sidings, being brought out only during the peak holiday season to make between ten and eighteen return trips, earning about £500,000 but costing between £3 and £4 million to maintain. Many rural train services carried fewer than a busload of passengers at any one time and lost more than twice the sum they took in fares. Suburban services were also making a loss. Even peak hour suburban services were being run at below their full operating cost. One fine example of the economic madness was the 06.50 service between Edinburgh and Berwick, which was studied by a Scottish newspaper in October 1961. In that month it cost £218 to run and took just £22 in fares. Only one person travelled on it for the full distance, and a handful of others for part of the way, but seventy-five railway staff used it for their free journeys to work.

The goods side was no better. Half of the freight stations produced less than 2 per cent of the total freight receipts. Freight wagons spent an average of 11.9 working days between picking up one load and the next (at a time when road hauliers were turning round cargoes in a matter of hours). The law also left them at a disadvantage. Until the Transport Act of 1962 they were statutory 'common carriers' – and therefore legally obliged to carry any cargo offered them, however unprofitable it might be; this left the competition free to skim off all the money-making items. By 1961, 40 per cent of all freight – once a virtual rail monopoly – had already shifted on to the roads. Coal was just about the only profitable rail traffic. This was despite the best efforts of the coal industry, which used the railway wagons as mobile coal bunkers, storing the coal in them for days at a time until it was required at the power stations. It was estimated that their 22 million wagon-days of storage per year cost the railways £11 million, for which the Coal Board paid just £1 million.

Small wonder that the railways lost some £960 million in the post-nationalisation years up to 1962. Efforts were already being made to turn the industry around – following the 1950s investment plan, the decade to 1962 saw the number of steam locomotives more than halved, diesel and electric locos increased ten-fold and staff cut by more than a quarter. But as early as 1960 Harold Macmillan said in the House of Commons that the railways needed some more radical modernisation. It was left to his Transport Minister – the extrovert ex-boxer, bookie's runner and self-made businessman Ernest Marples – to find the man to do it. Luckily, Marples had a close personal friend who fitted the bill.

Richard Beeching's wartime career was spent in the Armament Design Department of the Ministry of Supply (and anyone suggesting that he was responsible for the Bullet Train will be sent straight to their room). After the hostilities, he went to work for ICI, finally becoming a Technical Director on the main board. He served on the Stedeford Advisory Group, looking into the affairs of the British Transport Commission and, in June 1961, became the Chairman of the BTC, charged with reorganising the railways.

It was Beeching who rediscovered the lost secret of what railways were good at, and thus how they should be used. They had high fixed costs for their track. In 1961 it cost British Railways about £110 million – a quarter of their annual revenue – just to maintain it. This was before they provided any stations, sidings, locomotives or rolling stock. Against this, they could shift high volumes of goods and people in safety and comfort, and at relatively low unit cost. It was this high volume traffic that was the future of the railways, not the penny packets of custom on which much of the service then relied. Beeching staged a conference in York in April 1962

It was Beeching who rediscovered the lost secret of what railways were good at

Faith in the future. One characteristic of the 1960s was the faith in all things modern, be it the brutalism of new architecture and urban planning; new ways of shopping; or even the delights of the multi-storey car park!

Many a country line turned into a wild flower garden – with a little help from Dr Beeching.

at which he introduced the revolutionary concept of 'Organising the railways as a business'. This was followed in 1963 by the report called *The Reshaping of British Railways*. This set out to cut the unprofitable parts of the industry. The extent of the change it wrought can be seen from the following figures, describing the railways at the opposite ends of the decade:

	1960	1970
Route miles	18,369	11,799
Passenger and goods stations	7,283	2,868
Marshalling yards	876	146

Staffing levels similarly fell between 1961 and 1968, from just over 500,000 to just over 300,000.

Rural parts of the country suffered worst under the plan. For example, there were to be no trains to the north of Inverness, only one line through the heart of Wales, and radical cuts to coastal services along the north coast of Devon and Cornwall, around East Anglia and to the Lake District. Responses to the Beeching Plan were mixed and generally predictable. The Cabinet gave it qualified praise, calling it: 'An immensely competent document, as intricately technical as it is long.' The Labour shadow minister said the nation should be thankful to Dr Beeching for: 'One of the bravest efforts I have known in industry to face the economic facts of life.'

One surprise was the initial response of the train drivers' union, ASLEF, who described it as: 'An entirely honest attempt to rationalise the railway system. If it had been less ruthless, it would have been less honest.' However, normal service was resumed when the executive of the union rebuked their spokesman, 'vehemently repudiated' his views and called for

Residents of Newport Pagnell mourn the passing of their branch line.

industrial action to oppose much of the plan. Trades union fundamentalists saw it as a capitalist conspiracy, designed to drive traffic away from the nationalised railways and in to the arms of the privately owned road transport industry.

Battles were fought up and down the country by communities resisting the loss of their station or branch line. Many seaside towns forecast their imminent demise. The town clerk of St Ives was typical: 'I cannot see how the bus services could cope. We have nowhere to park the extra bus services.' (What about all that space where the railway station used to be?) Not every suggested closure was successful – the proposal to close Prime Minister Harold Wilson's constituency station of Huyton, for example, displayed more economic zeal than political acumen – and some services, which by purely economic criteria should have been closed in the 1960s, survive to this day.

Many of Beeching's opponents argued that his plan should not be put into practice until there had been an equally critical appraisal of road transport. Whether you believed this or not, it would have undoubtedly put off the evil day of closure for a good while. Dr Beeching himself had a good deal of sympathy for the idea. He said that he would like to give road freight an even more robust review than he had given the railways. He even went further:

> The railways are a very large, extreme and very visible example of the trouble that besets us in many facets of our national life. We have many sections of industry which for one reason or another are being propped up, and the longer we continue with this the

The railways try to woo the motorist.

BRITISH RAILWAYS
carries your freight

quickly, safely & reliably between anywhere

A daily door-to-door service between Great Britain and Ireland by British Railways provides fast, safe, regular and reliable freight transport to and from Northern Ireland via Heysham and Belfast. Geared to the London Midland Express Freight network, taking full advantage of the current modernisation programme, this service ensures prompt collection, rapid transport, prompt delivery (within 48 hours in most cases)—all at competitive rates.

New specially-designed container ships—*Container Enterprise* and *Container Venturer* —give regular overnight port-to-port trans-

port in all weathers. Combined with up-to-date shore handling equipment, these modern vessels help to maintain that regularity and reliability for which London Midland services are well-known.

Full details and rates for London Midland's Heysham-Belfast facilities are available from your Goods Agent or Station Master, or contact Station & Quay Superintendent, Heysham Harbour, Lancs. (Heysham 73) or Shipping Traffic Superintendent, 20 Donegall Quay, Belfast (Belfast 28061) or Irish Traffic Officer, Euston Station, London NW1 (Euston 1234 Ext. 526)

in Great Britain and anywhere in N. Ireland

The adverts spoke highly of them – but the reality was rather different.

deeper will be the difficulties that result and the more difficult will be the problems we shall have to solve. . . . In the next few years we shall find ourselves confronted very starkly with the necessity for reshaping the economy of this country in the most positive way.

SAVE YOUR RAILWAYS

A PUBLIC MEETING

Houldsworth Hall, Deansgate, Manchester
Sunday, 13th October, 1963, 3 p.m.

(Organised jointly by the Associated Society of Locomotive Engineers and Firemen, the National Union of Railwaymen, and the Transport Salaried Staffs' Association).

Speakers:

LORD STONHAM, O.B.E.
(National Council on Inland Transport)
WILLIAM BALLANTYNE
(Assistant General Secretary, National Union of Railwaymen)
HORACE NEWBOLD
(Manchester and Salford Trades Council)

Chair: **ELLIS SMITH, M.P.** (Stoke South)

Before the Meeting a Rally and Banner Procession. Assemble in Little Lever Street, off Hilton Street, Stevenson Square, at 2 p.m. Music by the Culcheth (Manchester) Military Band.

ACT NOW TO STOP RAIL CLOSURES

Groups around the country campaigned to save their local railway lines.

There were those among Beeching's admirers who thought his talents should be allowed a wider scope, for example reforming the Civil Service or the national economy itself.

One part of Beeching's work for the railways involved putting forward ideas about integrated forms of transport. For example, he

Modernisation of the railways was speeded up in the 1960s.

TO·DAY – MORE CITIES & TOWNS ARE SERVED BY DIESEL PULLMANS

THE MIDLAND PULLMAN
THE BIRMINGHAM PULLMAN : BUILT BY **METRO-CAMMELL**
THE BRISTOL PULLMAN

＊ TWO MORE DIESEL PULLMANS – TO·DAY

METROPOLITAN-CAMMELL CARRIAGE & WAGON CO. LTD.

HEAD OFFICE: SALTLEY · BIRMINGHAM 8   LONDON OFFICE: VICKERS HOUSE · BROADWAY · WESTMINSTER, S.W.1

argued that local authorities should not subsidise municipal bus companies to compete with under-used train services. Harold Wilson later asked him to undertake some further work for the government on the integration of different modes of transport. However, it was decided – with what some might see as supreme irony – that Beeching was too pro-rail and anti-road. He refused to be burdened with minders looking after the interests of the road haulage industry, and declined the job.

The railway closures became personally associated with Beeching, though he himself saw them very much as the work of a team. Resentment towards him was not helped by the fact that he was paid the equivalent of his ICI salary – £24,000 a year – for doing the job. The previous Railways Board chairman had been on £10,000, while a main line engine driver in 1960 earned a basic £676 a year for a 44-hour week.

Beeching left the railways in 1965 with a life peerage. He returned to ICI as Deputy Chairman and was also much in demand to sort out the problems of other businesses – even the Beatles approached him for help with some of their enterprises. He died – no doubt unlamented by trainspotters everywhere – at the age of seventy-one in 1985. His true monument is to be found in small towns around the country, where housing and other developments stand on the site of the town's demolished railway station. In places as far apart as Lincolnshire and Somerset, some wag has seen fit to name the street Beeching Close.

EXPORTS
to Northern Ireland and the Continent

'Drive-on drive-off'
Is quicker, easier, cheaper, safer

The drive-on drive-off ships of The Transport Ferry Service are the modern route across to Northern Ireland and the Continent. They're safer for your exports, the routes are simpler and you get faster deliveries. Lorries drive straight on to the ship from the quay and drive off again the other side. No loading and unloading. No handling delays. Breakages and pilfering are reduced to the minimum. Packaging is reduced and therefore safer. Road transport sailing from Tilbury or Preston *today* delivers your goods abroad *tomorrow!* Send your own lorries if they conform to international regulations, or write for names of haulage contractors operating through trunk services.

THE TRANSPORT FERRY SERVICE
(ATLANTIC STEAM NAVIGATION CO. LTD.)
25 WHITEHALL·LONDON·S.W.1·Telephone: WHitehall 6664 Telex 23482
REGULAR AND FREQUENT SAILINGS BETWEEN TILBURY AND ANTWERP
DAILY SAILINGS BETWEEN PRESTON AND NORTHERN IRELAND (LARNE OR BELFAST)

Road transport was already taking much of the railways' most lucrative business.

COME FLY WITH ME – AT A PRICE: CONCORDE

In the early months of 1960 a supersonic fighter plane reached Mach 2 (twice the speed of sound) in level flight for the first time. Even as the frontiers of science fiction were being rolled back, others were thinking about how ordinary members of the public might be conveyed at the same speed on a routine basis. The government had been working on supersonic aircraft since 1943 (before the first jet had even flown). Their initial programme was cancelled at the end of the war, but the Ministry of Supply had set up a committee in 1956 to consider the possibility of supersonic transport. They reported in 1959 that detailed research should be started on two 'first generation' supersonic planes. One would be capable of carrying 150 passengers between London and New York at Mach 2. The other was a 100 passenger aircraft capable of doing 1,500-mile journeys at Mach 1.2 (about 800mph). The cost would be substantial – the sum of £150 million was mentioned – and the market for such planes was limited. The short-haul version of the plane was soon discounted.

By November 1962 the British and French governments, and their respective aircraft industries, had signed agreements to develop a plane and in February 1965 construction work on the prototypes had begun. The treaty governing the project was deliberately drafted by the British without any break clauses, since the French had pulled out of an earlier joint effort. This backfired two years later, when the Labour government tried to borrow £900 million from the Americans. The Americans had always been keen to try to scupper the project, which had stolen a lead on its American rival, and they made the scrapping of the plane a condition of the loan. The Labour government discovered that withdrawal would leave them still liable for half the development costs, but unable to share in any of the commercial benefits. The French government would not even talk about withdrawal and the trades unions also lobbied hard against it –

Air traffic grew rapidly in the 1960s, allowing many more people to share the joys of waiting in the departure lounge.

not to mention the fact that withdrawal would probably have kissed goodbye to any chance we had of joining the Common Market. So this project went ahead, but many other areas of aeronautical research were dropped.

The costs steadily rose. By the end of 1967 the latest estimate was up to £500 million (half of it borne by Britain) and there was talk of the devaluation of the pound adding a further 14 per cent to that figure. In October 1968 a figure of £700 million was being whispered and the tabloid newspapers felt confident in rounding the eventual cost up to £1,000 million. By June 1973 the estimated cost had reached £1,065 million.

WHAT MAKES MY HEART GO BOOM?

The British Association for the Control of Aircraft Noise were also out to sink the project. They were unhappy with the tests the government had carried out to see whether people would put up with being deafened by a sonic boom – in the campaigners' view, sending a jet fighter over built-up areas at supersonic speed and then waiting to see how many people phoned in to complain was a fatuous way to conduct research. (Who do you phone, for one thing? *Yellow Pages* is completely silent on the subject of sonic booms.) But phone people did, and one of the more interesting findings was that the number of complaints was the same on days when bad weather caused the flights to be cancelled as on days when they flew. The cannons fired to welcome home round-the-world navigator Sir Francis Chichester provoked a flood of complaints about supersonic planes from irate Londoners. Another thing that made the protesters suspicious was the fact that many of the tests were conducted over the Bristol area, where the plane was to be made. Many of the potential complainants there might have seen it as a choice between boom or – as far as the local economy was concerned – bust. However, the fact that the tests took place over southern England did not prevent the authorities receiving one complaint from a keen-eared resident of Aberdeen.

Sonic booms were blamed for everything from broken bra straps to furniture shrinkage

The noise lobbyists wanted proper surveys done, like the ones being conducted by the Americans over Oklahoma. These brought in 4,000 complaints in a single month, with sonic booms blamed for everything from broken bra straps (one lady was allegedly left with no visible means of support eight times in one day) to furniture shrinkage. The French tests also brought their share of unlikely complaints: a farming family near Rennes, in Brittany, were killed when a sonic boom allegedly brought down the ceiling of their ancient farmhouse. The fact that they were storing eight tons of barley in the attic, resting on its antique roof timbers, was clearly quite unconnected with the fall.

The size of the boom problem was critical to the plane's success, since one of the key variables affecting the volume of the bang was the plane's size (and hence seating capacity). In the event it transpired that the boom was intolerable and the plane could not be flown over residential areas at supersonic speed.

DISCORDE OVER THE FRENCH LETTER

The two governments were discussing what the aircraft should be called. Early mock-ups had borne the name Super Caravelle, but this was clearly too French for British tastes. (Left to our own devices, we would probably have called it the Spitfire, especially if we had been building it with the Germans.) Officials from the two governments were toying with such uninspired names as Alliance and Europa, when the son of the British Aircraft Corporation's publicity manager came up with the idea of Concord(e). The Chairman of BAC liked it, and agreed it with his French counterpart without troubling the two governments by asking their views.

At this point a row broke out about how the name should be spelt – with the 'e', in the French manner, or without, in ours. Unhappily, the problem arose just at the time President de Gaulle was vetoing our entry to the Common Market, and this therefore became a vital matter of national pride. The French won. Technology Minister Tony Benn tried rather feebly to put a brave face on it, claiming that the 'e' stood for

British Concordes under construction at the Filton factory of the British Aircraft Corporation (now British Aerospace).

'excellence, England, Europe and the Entente'. Conservative MPs Ronald Bell and William Deedes were not convinced, and put a motion before the House of Commons that: 'This House notes with interest the Minister of Technology's attempt to be spry about his latest humiliating defeat at the hands of General de Gaulle and the French aircraft industry.' The letter E was henceforth known at BAC as 'the French letter'. The government ordered BAC to drop it from the name, which BAC refused to do. For the next five years all the BAC press handouts talked about Concorde, while those of the British government insisted on Concord. In case you had forgotten, the dictionary definition of the word concord is 'harmony, union'.

UNVEILING AND TEST FLIGHTS

Despite this, surveys in the trade press suggested that the commercial prospects for the plane were good. By the time the first prototype was wheeled out of its hangar in Toulouse in December 1967, it was claimed that sixteen airlines had placed seventy-four options to buy the plane. Fifteen of the sixteen sent their air hostesses, complete with special Concorde uniforms, to the ceremony.

The unveiling of the aircraft was one of those triumphs of Anglo-French co-operation that have been the hallmark of our nations' relationship since the Battle of Agincourt. Concorde was towed out in front of a forest of tricolors and one union jack. A French band made a mess of the British national anthem, while the Central Band of the RAF showed them how the Marseillaise should be played. The band then broke into the theme from *Those Magnificent Men in their Flying Machines* and the signature tune to the television puppet show *Thunderbirds*. The two governments' ministers each cut a ribbon. Officials were on hand, in case it became necessary to remove their scissors from their opposite numbers' backs afterwards.

The maiden flight was originally scheduled for early 1968, but the perfidious French tried to blame the delays on British non-delivery of engines. When they were forced to retract this vile slander, they made up some other reason why the British had caused the delay. By this time the British had scrapped the TSR2 military aircraft project. TSR2 shared engines with the Concorde, which meant that more of their development cost now fell on Concorde's, rather than the defence, budget. But by the time of the maiden flight, in March 1969, the industry had talked the sales potential up to ever greater levels. It was forecast that as many as 250 of the planes could be sold, bringing France and Britain an income of £2,000 million each. As the first flight got under way (after the wrong kind of wind threatened to delay it) advertisements appeared in the papers showing Concordes in the liveries of various airlines.

Some early demonstration models were painted in Air France colours on one side and British Airways livery on the other, so that xenophobic journalists could photograph the appropriate version. Rows used to break out on press days when the pilot flew past the press enclosure in one direction, but not in the other. Just to round off this joyous story of international co-operation, there was a further dispute when Concorde entered service, and it was discovered that the British pilots were being paid £14,000 a year, while their French counterparts were on £42,000.

Significantly, American manufacturers' initial interest in supersonic airliners had cooled considerably. They had originally opted for a much more ambitious 250-seater plane, travelling at Mach 3. Their Federal

The unveiling of the aircraft was one of those triumphs of Anglo-French co-operation that have been the hallmark of our nations' relationship since the Battle of Agincourt

The big, quick ones

Beirut. 2,300 miles. 90 minutes.
The Middle East, two leisurely
cigar smokes away. Time to read a magazine:
but only just.
This time-travelling schedule
is the fantastic promise of the Concorde.
And we've ordered two.

MEA
Middle East Airlines
LONDON 80 Piccadilly W 1 01-493 5681

*Two of the world's airlines that
promised their passengers a ride in
Concorde.*

Aviation Authority also predicted that it would be an all-economy class plane, on the assumption that most first-class passengers would have their own private jets by the 1970s. When they finally cancelled plans for the Boeing SST in 1970, optimists added another hundred to the potential market for Concorde.

Thereafter, the main threat to Concorde in the market-place was felt to come from 'Concordski' – the Russian Tupolev TU144 Charger, a Concorde lookalike that had beaten them into the air by making its maiden flight on New Year's Eve 1968. In the event the Russian version turned out to have serious flaws in its design, and it disappeared from the skies after just a few commercial trips and a very public crash in front of 300,000 people at the Paris Air Show. This particular crash was not thought to have originated from a technical fault, but there was also another, less publicised, accident in service in Russia – and there may have been a darker side to the aircraft's failure. It is known that the Russians were

Air Canada's Concordes will land you in Montreal 3 hours before you leave London

Actual flight time 3 hours! But with the help of supersonic speeds and the 6-hour difference between London and Montreal local time, passengers could leave London at 10.00 am and arrive at 7.00 am in Montreal.

AIR CANADA

142/4 Regent Street, London, W.1. 01-829 7233
And Glasgow, Birmingham, Manchester, Leeds, Dublin and Shannon.

THE ADVERTISER, FRIDAY, FEBRUARY 5, 1960

INCLUSIVE PRICES from LONDON MANCHESTER & BIRMINGHAM

BLUE CARS

CONTINENTAL HOLIDAYS

CENTRE Holidays by AIRLINER, RECLINING-SEAT COACH, ALL-COUCHETTE TRAIN ! Grand Scenic Coach Tours, Luxury Sea Cruises ! **PLUS** CONFIDENTIAL CREDIT FACILITIES giving 6, 9 or 12 months to pay (very modest terms). Here are a few examples from **OVER 500** Blue Cars Holiday Bargains . . .

OBERAMMERGAU 12 Days with KITZBUHEL including GUARANTEED Seat at PASSION PLAY **28½** GNS By COACH	Sunny **SAN SEBASTIAN** 12 DAYS **29½** GNS By AIR
10 Days Holiday with A WEEK at **LAKE LUCERNE** BERNESE OBERLAND AUSTRIA, GERMANY, SPAIN • • • from **18½** GNS BY COACH	**COSTA BRAVA** 15 DAYS **34** GNS By AIR
15 DAYS Grand **ITALIAN** COACH TOUR ROME · FLORENCE · VENICE · CAPRI **65** GNS	**MAJORCA** 15 DAYS • By AIR **39** GNS
10 and **17** DAY HOLIDAYS · · BY ALL-COUCHETTE SPECIAL TRAIN · · · · to OBERAMMERGAU AUST. TYROL, ITALIAN ADRIATIC RIVIERA, YUGOSLAVIA, SWITZERLAND and GERMANY from **£21**/17/0	**LUGANO** 14 DAYS **36½** GNS BY COACH

APPOINTED BLUE CARS AGENTS

ASHLEY ADAMS

(MACCLESFIELD) LTD.

16 Chestergate . Macclesfield

Telephone 3758

R.M.S Andes 27,000 tons

The Cruise of a Lifetime

'NOTHING BUT THE BEST for people who *know*' is the keynote of a cruise with Royal Mail Lines. Flawlessly planned in every detail for the discriminating passenger, every Royal Mail cruise offers memorable weeks of pleasure replete with every luxury. 'Andes' is air-conditioned throughout and fitted with stabilisers. Each cabin has its own bathroom or shower, and the single spacious Dining Saloon enables all the passengers to dine together.

The discriminating passenger knows that a capacity of only 500 passengers on a ship of 27,000 tons means spaciousness and comfort.

Come cruising with Royal Mail—the line that couldn't care *more* for those who care about comfort. There are cruises calling at the nicest places under the sun . . .

CRUISE No. 1 21 days (June 10–July 1) Accommodation **available** from £266.
Calling at Gibraltar, Naples (for Rome, Pompei, Amalfi & Sorrento), Rhodes, Barcelona (for Monserrat & Costa Brava), Lisbon (for Sintra & Estoril).
CRUISE No. 4 14 days (Aug. 14–Aug. 28) Accommodation **available** from £177.
Calling at Vigo (for La Toja & Santa Tecla), Spezia (for Pisa, Florence & Italian Riviera), Lisbon (for Sintra & Estoril).
CRUISE No. 5 20 days (Sept. 3–Sept. 23) Accommodation **available** from £253.
Calling at Gibraltar, Villefranche (for Nice, Monte Carlo, Cannes & Grasse), Venice, Dubrovnik, Kotor, Lisbon (for Sintra & Estoril).
Please contact your Travel Agent or our Cruising Department T.3.

ROYAL MAIL LINES

ROYAL MAIL HOUSE, LEADENHALL ST., LONDON, E.C.3. TEL: MAN 0522 OR AMERICA HOUSE, COCKSPUR STREET, LONDON, S.W.1. TEL: WHI 3640

Holidays Ahead

with Wallace Arnold

Over 75,000 enjoyed a Wallace Arnold holiday last year. The 1960 Programme is Bigger and Better than ever before : read about the galaxy of holidays personally planned for YOU . there are courier-conducted coach holidays throughout Britain and the Continent, there are all-inclusive holidays by Air or all-couchette Britannia Express—holidays that get you straight to your chosen resort and leave you fancy free to enjoy your holiday . Send for the beautifully illustrated Holiday Brochure to help you plan the holiday of your dreams.

Three Magnificent Holiday Programmes

BRITISH COACH HOLIDAYS		CONTINENTAL COACH HOLIDAYS		CONTINENTAL HOLIDAYS BY AIR or RAIL NEW for you in 1960	
4,5 & 7 Days DEVON & TORQUAY	11 GNS	12 Days GRAND SWISS	51 GNS	8 or 15 Days by Air SAN REMO from £8.10.0	44 GNS
7 Days GREAT GLENS	23½	12 Days FRENCH RIVIERA	55½	7 or 14 Days by Air or Rail LUCERNE	30½
7 Days DEESIDE	23½ GNS	10 Days LAUSANNE	41	7 or 14 Days by Air DINARD	23
7 Days TROSSACHS	23½ GNS	10 Days INTERLAKEN	39½	7 or 14 Days by Air or Rail MONTREUX	30½
7 Days ISLE OF BUTE	23½ GNS	11 Days LUGANO	53½	7 or 14 Days by Air or Rail VENICE LIDO	34 GNS
9 Days SKYE	31½	12 Days 6 COUNTRIES	55½	7 or 14 Days by Air MAJORCA	39 GNS
14 Days JOHN O'GROATS	47½	8,10 or 15 Days NORWAY	43 GNS	7 or 14 Days by Air or Rail CATTOLICA	28½ GNS
7 Days WALES	22½ GNS	12 Days OBERAMMERGAU	53 GHS	7 or 14 Days by Air TOSSA DE MAR	36 GNS
7 Days CORNISH RESORTS	22½ GNS	7 Days BELGIUM	26½ GNS	7 or 14 Days by Air or Rail FORTE DEI MARMI	34 GNS
10 Days FALMOUTH & SCILLY ISLES	33	9 Days HOLLAND	32½ GNS	7 or 14 Days by Air or Rail KITZBUHEL	31½
10 Days IRELAND	40 GNS	14 Days Idyllic ITALY	74½	7 or 14 Days by Air CAPRI or SORRENTO 7 or 14 days in RESORT	53 GNS

WALLACE ARNOLD TOURS LTD.

Book At Your Local Travel Agent

R. M. ADAMS Travel Agency

31, KINGSBURY SQUARE,   AYLESBURY.   TELEPHONE 3121

Package holidays make going abroad as cheap as staying at home.

actively trying to steal technical secrets from British aircraft manufacturers – Yevgeny Ivanov, the Russian spy at the centre of the Profumo scandal, admitted to stealing an aircraft part from the Farnborough Air Show, for example. The British spy Greville Wynne later claimed that a Russian mole was found inside the BAC plant in Bristol and was deliberately fed misinformation that led to the TU144's downfall – literally.

In technological terms, at least, our plane did everything that was expected of it. Asked how the first British test flight had gone, test pilot Brian Trubshaw said 'It was wizard.' Even then, three years before it was to enter service, BOAC had 274 bookings for early flights on a plane they had not even ordered yet. The British finally placed an order, for five aircraft, in May 1972, with the French signing up for four shortly afterwards.

The trouble was, nobody else did. When the last production Concorde left Bristol in April 1979, just fourteen models had been sold, seven each to British Airways and Air France. Not only did they lose money for the governments and manufacturers, but it was forecast at the time of their delivery that British Airways' first five Concordes would have an annual operating loss of £25 million. The only person who thought he could make them pay was the cut-price airline king Freddie Laker. A technological triumph, and one of the most beautiful planes in aviation history (unless you happened to live under its flightpath), Concorde had turned out to be a commercial blind alley.

The only person who thought he could make them pay was the cut-price airline king Freddie Laker

LAST OF THE QUEENS

Up to the 1950s, anyone wishing to travel between Europe and America had little choice but to go by sea. Fleets of liners carried the vast majority of the business and leisure traffic between the two continents. The post-war peak in passenger liner traffic came in the mid-1950s, when over a million passengers a year were carried across the ocean. By the 1960s the passenger trade had dropped dramatically, to around 600,000 a year, while transatlantic air traffic was increasing at 15 per cent per annum, from 1 to 5 million annually. The new growth market for the shipping companies was for cruise vessels. It was during this period of transition that Cunard directors were trying to plan the replacements for their ageing Queens, *Mary* and *Elizabeth*. Before that time, the design brief for a new liner was relatively simple – you simply made the new vessel larger and faster than the one it was replacing. Cunard started down this road in the late 1950s with the Q3 project, a 75,000-ton passenger transport, on which the metaphorical plug was pulled just in time.

The cruise vessel market was different. First, speed was not such an essential. A fast, large ship is expensive to run and holiday passengers are by no means in the same hurry as those simply trying to get from A to B. Second, the economies of scale involved in delivering vast numbers of people across the Atlantic ceased to apply. It became increasingly difficult to keep all the spaces filled as the non-leisure traffic drifted away to the airlines. There were also other, more subtle, differences in design. With a passenger transport, the aim is to make it feel as much like a hotel and as little like a ship as possible, to minimise the sensation of being at sea. With a cruise liner, being on board ship is part of the novelty of the holiday and needs to be exploited to the full.

Then there were the changes that were taking place in class attitudes. On an old-fashioned passenger liner, there had to be strict demarcation between the classes of travellers (as any viewer of the film *Titanic* will recall) to stop the hoi polloi mixing with those of us with culture and breeding. On a cruise liner, where passengers are on board much longer, variety is everything, and passengers need to be allowed to roam the length of the ship to find it. (At least you can be assured that you will only mix with the rich hoi polloi.) The new boat was therefore conceived as a three-class ship, launched as a two-class ship and, when cruising, now operates as one-class. These were some of the factors that Cunard were trying to juggle with as they placed their order for the new (as yet un-named) ship in December 1964. Such was their commitment to it that they sold their stake in BOAC (the forerunner to British Airways) to help pay for it – a move not appreciated by all of their shareholders.

The concept tended to change as they went along, but what they ended up with was a 58,000-ton ship carrying 2,005 passengers and 760 crew. There were to be four swimming pools, three restaurants and 6,000 square yards of deck for the passengers to spread themselves out on. For those travellers who were joined to their cars at the hip, there were even enough car parking spaces on board for the ship to be classified by the RAC as a car ferry (the only one to be given five stars by them). The contract price for the project, named Q4, was £25.4 million, to which the government contributed a loan of £17.6 million. Early problems led to a six-month delay in the launching, and the price rapidly escalated in the direction of

The QE2 has her aluminium superstructure fitted.

143

'I name this ship . . . er, me.'
Her Majesty launches the QE2,
20 September 1967.

£30 million. The company sought further help from the government, whose investment by the time of launching grew to £24 million out of the estimated £29 million cost.

But never mind! It was almost entirely British-built and contained the most advanced computer system of any merchant ship of its time. The £100,000 Ferranti Argos 400 computer, again mostly paid for with public money, did everything from navigating to ordering the scampi for the restaurants and totting up the passengers' bar bills. If my experience of computers is anything to go by, this probably meant that the captain got an awful lot of bar bills and that the scampi were ordered to steer the boat.

The Q4 became the *Queen Elizabeth II* when she was launched in September 1967 in front of an estimated crowd of 100,000. It took a further eighteen months to get her ready for her maiden voyage, with 2,000 men working on her. She was delayed and her first voyage was a tentative one, covering the 13 miles from Clydebank to Greenock at a cautious 7 knots, with Prince Charles on her bridge. Testing revealed serious problems with her steam turbines and Cunard refused to accept delivery of their new flagship. Her maiden voyage had to be cancelled, at a cost to Cunard of $10 million. It was not until May 1969 that she was

A youthful Prince Charles joins the Captain for the QE2's maiden voyage.

The QE2 arrives in New York after her maiden voyage in May 1969.

able to set out on her maiden voyage to New York. The first crossing saw the ship's first christening and first funeral – a steward, who died en route and was buried at sea. The modern interior decor of the new Queen came as a shock to some passengers who had been used to the traditional liners, and some felt she did not quite match up to the highest standards of her predecessors. As one commentator put it, after the maiden voyage: 'More Carlton Tower than Savoy; brassy, rather than serene.'

When she was first launched, you could enjoy a five-day crossing of the Atlantic – tourist class – for as little as $255. Today, if you wanted

THE AUSTIN A40

The shape isn't just pretty to look at...
it makes sense

It's a distinctive shape, the A40. A shape designed for the best
and simplest of reasons: it makes sense. Move the fully folding
back seat down and there's extra space for a mountain of
luggage. Or, with the back seat up, you get a normal-sized
boot that's *inside* the car. Then check the price: £460 plus
£96.7.11 P.T. . . . £556.7.11. It makes sense to invest yourself with an Austin A40.

you **invest** *in an* **AUSTIN** *at*

IVOR F. MILES
SALES AUSTIN SERVICE
CHURCHWAY, HADDENHAM—Telephone 263
Also a good selection of Guaranteed Used Cars

MOTOR CARS & COMMERCIAL VEHICLES FOR SALE

BEDFORD
12-seaters

There's a passenger-carrying Bedford to suit your
purpose—fast, smooth and sturdy—with the road-
ability and parkability of a saloon car.
Lively, economical 'over-square' engine, all-synchro-
mesh gearbox, ball-bearing steering, heavy-duty
tyres and rear springs.
Luxury models for family and business travel.
Tough, workaday models for industrial service.
Ask for free, illustrated catalogues.

UTILABRAKE £602   WORKOBUS £551
(Long wheelbase £632)   *(Long wheelbase £576)*

MOORES and NEWTON
LTD.
Sales Wilmslow 4932
8 a.m. — 6 p.m.   MONDAY — SATURDAY

---

*Car manufacturers in the 1960s anticipated many of the fashions
of later years. There were hatchbacks, people carriers, sports
saloons, minis of every description . . . and extremely long cars,
bought by midgets if the illustration is to be believed.*

to make the crossing in real style, you could end up with no change out of $10,000. Over the years Cunard have spent over six times the original cost of the ship on five major and two minor refits. She has had new engines, changed superstructure, new interior decor, new paintwork – even a new funnel. The *QE2* went to the Falklands as a troopship and has also sailed through the 130mph winds and 90ft waves of a hurricane. She has made over a thousand crossings of the Atlantic.

CHRONICLE OF THE 1960s:
TRANSPORT LANDMARKS

1960: Britax manufacture the first inertia reel seatbelts.

12 September 1960: First MoT tests for cars over ten years old.

27 September 1960: First travelator opens at the Bank Underground station.

5 February 1961: First automatic half-barrier level crossing at Uttoxeter, Staffordshire.

6 March 1961: First minicabs introduced.

8 May 1962: Last London trolley-bus.

28 October 1962: First urban motorway: the Stretford–Eccles by-pass.

1962: First self-service petrol filling station, Southwark Bridge, London.

1963: The 'A' registration suffix is introduced. (It is not used in all areas until 1965.)

1964: First electronic ticket barrier on the Underground and first unmanned trains on the Central Line.

April 1964: First commercial hydrofoil service, between the Channel Islands and France.

10 June 1965: First automatic aeroplane landing, by a BEA Trident travelling from Paris to Heathrow.

24 November 1965: Experimental 70mph limit on motorways announced.

1965: First Panda cars.

8 September 1966: The Queen opens the Severn Bridge.

21 March 1968: Breathalyser cuts road deaths by 23 per cent in its first three months.

14 October 1968: The Queen opens Euston station.

9 February 1969: The Boeing 747 Jumbo jet makes its maiden flight, near Seattle. (It enters commercial service in January 1970.)

The new-fangled motorways turn out to breed more traffic.

CHAPTER 11

FROM RACHMAN TO RONAN: HOUSING IN THE 1960s

At the earliest moment, local authorities should be required to submit a building programme for 5 or 10 years to come, based on a systematic plan to deal with slums and with acute overcrowding.

Enoch Powell, in the days of 'one nation' Conservative housing policy

Housing was one of the big political issues of the 1950s and 1960s. Even before the Second World War, Britain had faced a huge backlog of sub-standard housing, with some 550,000 houses classified as slums and awaiting demolition, and a further 350,000 on the borderline. All house-building stopped with the outbreak of war, though Hitler carried on with the clearance programme, demolishing 475,000 properties (unfortunately, not always the right ones) and damaging many others. The war also added to demand, with a flood of some 2 million wartime marriages, a baby boom and a steady market for single person housing thereafter, as divorce rose steadily among those who had married in rather too much haste during the blackout. Add to this massive amounts of internal migration, as old industries declined and people went in search of new work, and the demands of foreign servicemen, refugees and ex-prisoners of war, and you had a full-blown post-war housing crisis.

Hitler carried on with the clearance programme, demolishing 475,000 properties and damaging many others

Despite the strenuous efforts of the governments of the 1950s, they scarcely kept up with the numbers of houses falling into disrepair, which still totalled 824,000 by 1965. The new Labour government in 1964 set itself a target of trying to build 500,000 per year. They did not quite manage it, but more housing was built in Britain in the five years to 1970 than in any similar period since the First World War.

Not everyone had housing problems. This woman even got Green Shield trading stamps with her house purchase.

CATHY COME HOME

On 16 November 1966 a 65-minute play was broadcast by the BBC. It was written by Jeremy Sandford and based on his own experience of homelessness, and was to become one of the most influential broadcasts in the history of television. *Cathy Come Home* was directed by Ken Loach. It told the story of a young couple, Cathy and Reg, and their children. In the course of the play their financial and housing situation goes steadily from bad to worse. They become homeless, split up and the final traumatic scene shows the children being torn from the arms of their mother and taken into care. The play attracted an audience of about 12 million, half as many again as the average for a Wednesday play. It pushed housing up the political agenda and encouraged the formation of the housing charity Shelter. When it was reshown in 1968, it also led to the launch of the London Squatters' Campaign, which revived tactics used by the homeless at the end of the Second World War. The anarchist left seized upon squatting as a way of creating an alternative society. Their attitudes created tensions with the more mainstream squatters, and led to the police and the Greater London Council breaking up some squats.

One of the most highly publicised of these was the occupation of 144 Piccadilly. In September 1969 a large group of squatters occupied this hundred-room mansion near Park Lane. It had been vacant, pending demolition by its owners, Amalgamated West End Developments. At one point in the first week, several hundred so-called hippies were resident. Some of them, such as Dr Mary Glavin (her PhD from the University of California, Berkeley, naturally), sat on mattresses for the benefit of visiting hacks, singing *Where have all the flowers gone?* and explaining that they were only stopping temporarily, as part of a Europe-wide tour of peace and harmony. Others had longer-term plans for residence. One, known only as 'Dr John' (his PhD, one suspects, from the University of Life, Faculty of Hard Knocks) announced his intention to turn the house into a base for underground groups and a home for some of London's homeless families. The end came within a week of their occupation. Watched by a crowd of some 2,000 sightseers, a first wave of about fifty police went in the front way, and were subjected to a hail of water-filled balls, roofing tiles and other missiles hurled by the 200 or so squatters left in there. More police went in through the back, as the sightseers assisted the police (or possibly just joined in the fun) by picking up the missiles and hurling them back into the building. It was over within a few minutes. Some thirty of the occupants were charged with a combination of drugs and public order offences. Eight 'aliens' (presumably from other parts of this planet) were seized and a number of minors were returned to their family homes 'in need of a good bath'. There were complaints that the building had been damaged, for example through the painting of graffiti on the walls (which seems a little churlish, considering it was about to be demolished). A grateful developer called at the police station later and paid £1,000 into the Police Benevolent Fund. It was probably cheaper than hiring the man at the centre of the next section.

A number of minors were returned to their family homes 'in need of a good bath'

RACHMAN

Immediately after the war almost 60 per cent of households lived in private rented accommodation. The spectacular decline of this sector, which formed just 9 per cent of the housing stock by 1977, was one of the major developments in post-war housing. To prevent profiteering in a scarce market, rent controls had been introduced on many privately let properties after the war. This limited their rents to twice their immediately pre-war level. The Conservative governments of the 1950s became concerned at the decline of the private rented sector and introduced a new Rent Act in 1957. This immediately removed controls on about 810,000 higher value properties and allowed 'creeping decontrol' of a further 4.3 million. As a property was vacated, its rent could be fully decontrolled, and could rise to whatever the market would bear. This did not have the intended effect of increasing investment in the rented sector. It simply encouraged many landlords to obtain vacant possession and sell. It also contributed to one of the great housing scandals of the 1960s.

One man came to be personified as the symbol of all the bad landlords during this period. His activities were to lead to an independent inquiry into housing in London and to changes in the law. Peter (Perec) Rachman was born in Poland in 1919 and as a Jew he suffered persecution both from the Nazis and in a Stalinist labour camp. He washed up in England as a refugee in 1946 and spent time in various camps here. Experiences like these might have led him to identify with those who found themselves disadvantaged and in housing need, but they seemed to have quite the opposite effect on him.

He became a scorer at Jack Solomon's billiard hall in Soho. It was there that he started his involvement with property, helping prostitutes to find rooms. By 1953 he was acquiring properties all over London. His progress was helped by a number of factors. First was the huge wave of West Indian immigration after the war. Many landlords would not even consider black tenants and it was left to the likes of Rachman to put a roof – however inadequate and over-priced – over their heads. Moreover, Rachman was not above deliberately putting some of his more boisterous West Indian tenants into any of his houses with 'difficult' residents, who would not take Rachman's hints that it was time for them to move.

It was estimated that in the early 1960s some two million properties nationally had rents that were controlled. If the tenants of these could be removed, the property could either be sold, at several times its tenanted value, or it could be let out to groups – like the West Indian immigrants – who either did not know their rights or could easily be persuaded not to exert them. The 1957 Rent Act, discussed earlier, made it possible for them to be decontrolled rather more easily, and the opposition lost no time in laying much of the blame for Rachmanism at the door of the government.

Rachman used to send round the 'soft glove gang' whenever he wanted a tenant to depart. They would start with gentle hints, like taking the tenant's furniture into the street and chopping it up into small pieces. If the tenant failed to take the hint, they might take up the floorboards. The process might then move on to direct physical intimidation or violence, for the benefit of the really insensitive occupier. Rachman had various ways of making life unpleasant – a blocked drain could be left for months to create a health hazard. Any effort to enlist the help of the local authority to get it fixed would be buried in a web of confusion and deceit, as Rachman and the agents who fronted his operation moved properties between the various companies that represented his interests. All sorts of extortionate practices were employed by Rachman and his fellow rogue landlords. They would charge a new tenant £25 key money and then, a week later, issue them with notice to quit. Some even charged a £25 viewing fee for the flat, with no refund if the prospective tenant chose not to take it. They would charge for pets – one woman bought a tank of tropical fish and found her rent increased by 5s a week. A tenant might be told that two months' rent was required up front. The following month, a different rent collector would show up, saying that the property had been sold on, and that the new landlord had nothing to do with any arrangement the tenant might have made with the old one. Gross overcrowding was commonplace. A seven-roomed house might have forty immigrants sleeping in it in shifts, each paying £1 a week rent.

Conditions like these became public knowledge well before the Notting Hill race riots of the late 1950s, but the government, the police and local authorities were all slow to respond. The National Federation of Property Owners tried to put the blame on rent control itself. There was, they said,

One woman bought a tank of tropical fish and found her rent increased by 5s a week

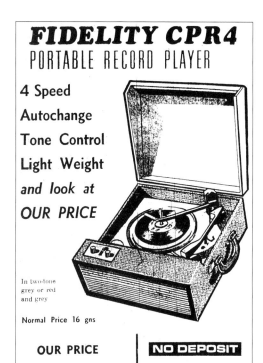

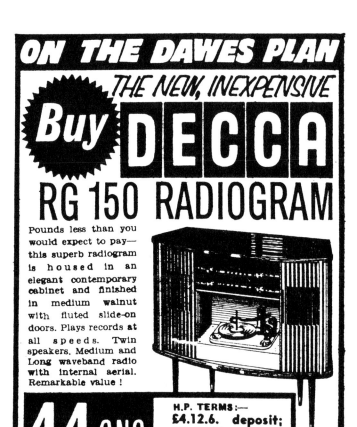

Ideal Homes 1960s-style record players, radiograms, plastic furniture and washing machines.

little profit to be made from evicting someone who was already paying market rent. But so long as there were properties whose rents remained at about half the market level through rent control, there would always be easy pickings for those who were prepared to use illegal means to get the controlled tenants out. Their position was supported by rabid Members of Parliament, such as Mr Rees-Davies (Conservative, Thanet) who claimed that the opposition's complaints about the likes of Rachman in the House were based on information provided by communists and criminals.

Local authorities were hamstrung in various ways. In addition to the usual lack of resources, there was the unwillingness of tenants to come forward with information, especially if it meant giving evidence in court and then going home on a dark night without a police escort. There was also the difficulty of picking your way through the ever-shifting maze of interlocking ownerships to serve notice on the real owner of the property. In addition, there was a suggestion that some of the London councils were ideologically ill-disposed to interfering. As a spokesman for Kensington Council put it: 'We do not and cannot employ hundreds of snoopers, nor is our function that of agent provocateur.' They would far rather wait for complaints to come in to them. As for the police, there were suggestions that a number of key officers were uncomfortably close friends with Rachman and his money.

In addition to his property interests, Rachman was involved in all sorts of other unpleasantness. He was personally a voracious user of women and was involved in prostitution rackets. He was an associate of Stephen Ward, and both Christine Keeler and Mandy Rice-Davies were at one time or another his mistresses. His hired thugs were involved in murder and (after his death) supplied the guns for the Spaghetti House siege. He also ran clubs, moving in the same gangland circles as the Krays and the Richardsons. By the late 1950s he was a seriously wealthy man. It was said that his slum property alone was bringing him in £78,000 a year. He could afford to indulge his taste for high living and had plans for 'going legitimate'. This would involve selling off his slum property to surrogate owners and investing heavily in property that was about to be acquired for the building of the M6 motorway.

His plans were not to materialise. Rachman died in November 1962, suffering a massive heart attack at the age of forty-two. He was supposed to have been hugely rich (never having paid tax) but after his death they found only £72,800 in traceable assets and this was more than wiped out by liabilities. Some thought that he had salted his millions away in foreign bank accounts, but his family apparently spent as much time searching for the missing millions as did the taxman.

Rachman's real notoriety only really came out after his death. His widow complained at the campaign of posthumous vilification that was heaped on him. The public outcry against Rachmanism led to the setting up of an independent inquiry into housing in London, under Sir Milner Holland QC, and in 1964 new powers were given to local authorities to take over the running of properties where the tenants were being given the Rachman treatment. The scandal of Rachmanism led to the reintroduction of rent control, once a Labour government was installed, and to the Fair Rent legislation of 1965. But one effect of this was to make private renting

The public outcry against Rachmanism led to the setting up of an independent inquiry into housing in London

increasingly unprofitable for landlords. In addition the clearance programmes continued to eat into the stock of private rented property. Over the next decade or so the supply of rented accommodation fell to less than 10 per cent of the total housing stock.

RONAN POINT

High-rise buildings, using prefabricated techniques, became popular during the 1960s. They were claimed to be relatively inexpensive, efficient in their use of both labour and land, and quick to erect. A twenty-storey block of a hundred or more flats could be put up in as little as eighteen months. Governments preoccupied with the housing numbers game put a lot of pressure on local authorities to adopt them as a major plank in their housing programmes. One such system was a Danish design, built under licence in Britain by the construction company Taylor Woodrow. It was a tried and tested system which had been around since 1948. Some 35,000 examples of such buildings were to be found across

Central government put pressure on local authorities to build high . . . but some blocks were demolished even before they had been paid for.

Europe, and schemes using it had won a Civic Trust award for the Greater London Council. So the London Borough of Newham felt confident in using it to help tackle their vast housing problem. They invested £2.1 million in four high-rise blocks in Canning Town. One of these was a 23-storey block of 110 flats named Ronan Point. It was virtually new – only 80 of the flats were occupied and none of the residents had been there for more than two months.

At about 6.00 a.m. one May morning in 1968 a huge explosion ripped through a flat on the eighteenth floor of Ronan Point. The entire corner of the building collapsed – the term everybody used was 'like a house of cards'. Terrified residents – some still in their night clothes – fled down the many flights of stairs, since the lifts cut off automatically in an emergency. Fortunately few people had been in their living rooms that early in the morning, and it had been those rooms that had given way. Of the 260 residents, only 3 were initially reported dead. The toll was eventually to rise to 5, with another 17 injured.

The government immediately promised a public inquiry into the disaster, and the manufacturers launched their own separate investigation into what had gone wrong. The residents had some questions of their own about the safety of the flats when it emerged, for example, that they were twice as tall as the highest escape ladder owned by the Fire Brigade. Others, however, had greater faith in high-rise living. About a dozen of the families evacuated from the ruins of Ronan Point moved directly into Merrit Point, an identical building in the same development.

Other local authorities also started looking nervously at their own high-rise buildings. The Greater London Council, for example, had no fewer than thirty-three such blocks under construction. The inquiry established that some 400 to 500 buildings, occupied by 25,000

The change came too late for the residents of Ronan Point.

families and owned by 73 local authorities, were affected nationwide. As for the cause of the explosion, the man from the gas board put it down to 'a rogue nut' – the crucial kind of nut that held the gas pipe on to the back of the cooker. The problem with the faulty nut had apparently been compounded by the amateur gasfitter who had connected Mrs Ivy Hodge's gas cooker for her, up on the eighteenth floor.

Authorities were advised by the government – rather superfluously, one might think – to shut off gas supplies to system-built blocks if they found any sign of progressive collapse in them. Newham Council decided to take no chances, and made arrangements to issue each of their high-rise tenants affected with a free £40 electric cooker. One of the tenants complained – she was scared stiff of electricity, ever since getting an electric shock. Didn't they realise how dangerous it was?

The five people killed were not the last victims of the disaster. Shortly afterwards, Taylor Woodrow announced the redundancy of forty of its workers at its system building

factory. But, they were at pains to assure the world, the fall-off in demand for system-built housing was nothing whatsoever to do with the collapse of Ronan Point.

Ronan Point can be seen as a watershed in society's attitude to high-rise building – at least as a solution to mass family housing needs. High-rise had originally been used, from the 1930s onwards, by well-off – and predominantly childless – couples. It was, and remains, popular with these groups, for whom it can be built and maintained to a sufficiently high standard. But local authorities are forever being forced to cut costs, and this tells in both the original specification and the standard of maintenance of municipal high-rises. Despite their claimed cheapness of construction, they proved to be expensive to maintain, with troublesome lifts, rubbish chutes and other communal areas. In some cases the additional cost of installing a concierge proved to be an essential part of the war against vandalism. Many of the prefabricated systems also proved to have serious flaws (apart from the tendency to collapse like a house of

*Home comforts such as central
heating and double glazing were
slow to catch on. Some people
thought them 'cissy'.*

cards). Poor heating, inadequate insulation, condensation, cracking concrete and cladding that had an alarming tendency to fall off were all parts of the joys of tower block living up and down the country.

Even the claims that had originally been made for high-rise turned out to be false. All the systems proved to be at least twice as expensive per square foot to build as conventional housing and even the speed of construction did not stand up to scrutiny. With low-rise housing, each unit can be occupied individually as it is completed. With a tower block, you had to wait for the whole development, of maybe a hundred units, to be completed. Viewed in these terms, average times from start to occupation could be higher than for conventional housing.

The late 1960s saw a radical shift away from the 'mass clearance' approach to urban renewal – helped in part by the fact that many of the very worst slums had by then gone. Government policy changed to one of active discouragement of high-rise. A new Housing Act saw a move away from large-scale redevelopment to a more selective approach, combining redevelopment with General Improvement Areas and Housing Action Areas, through which both existing properties and their surroundings could be renovated. Instead, the attention of the bulldozers turned to much newer creations. By the late 1970s authorities like Birkenhead were beginning to demolish tower blocks that had become unlettable, some of them forty years before they would even be paid for.

In addition to the new estates that had replaced slum housing on inner city sites, some real horror stories were to be found in some of the overspill estates that surrounded many of our major cities. Kirkby, outside Liverpool, the home of *Z Cars*, was a good example. Planned as a 'complete community', with an industrial estate of 750 acres, about 50,000 people moved there. While full employment lasted, all was relatively well. But as the local economy collapsed, it became a horror story of crime, dereliction and social problems, the people isolated from many of the traditional community networks that helped other parts of Liverpool to endure hard times.

Assertive 1960s womanhood breaks down the old taboos – like these two protesters occupying a men-only bar, and this pack assaulting the male bastion of rugby union.

CHRONICLE OF THE 1960s:
THE TRIUMPHS OF WOMANHOOD

1960: The first Playboy club opens, providing feminists around the world with ammunition for their outrage.

1960: Sirimavo Bandaranaike of Ceylon becomes the world's first woman Prime Minister after her husband was assassinated by a Buddhist monk.

8 October 1962: The first female High Court judge: Elizabeth Lane.

1964: The world's first topless waitress, Carol Doda, appears at the Condor Beach Club, San Francisco.

10 June 1965: The first female member of the Stock Exchange: Mrs C.V. Ward.

20 June 1966: the first woman to fly solo around the world, Sheila Scott, lands her Piper Comanche at Heathrow after a 33-day trip.

April 1967: The first female London cabbie: Mrs Shirley Preston.

13 November 1969: Quintuplets are born to Mrs Irene Hanson of Rayley, Essex, following fertility treatment.

Women's work – in the days when you were still allowed to call it that.

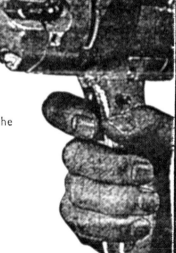

CHAPTER 12

BAD BOYS: SOME VILLAINS OF THE 1960s

Ronnie does some funny things.

Reggie Kray's reaction to the news that
his brother had murdered George Cornell

In this final chapter, we look at some of the villains of the decade. One who would undoubtedly have qualified for membership of this band – Peter Rachman – has already made his appearance under his own specialised subject, in the housing chapter.

THE KRAYS

Twins Ronnie and Reggie Kray, and their elder brother Charles, were possibly the most feared members of London's underworld during the 1960s. Their criminal gang, the Firm, collected protection money, organised illegal gambling and drinking clubs and waged deadly gang warfare. But according to Mrs Kate Kray, Ronnie's second wife, he was always immaculate in his dress sense, a perfect gentleman and devoted to his mother, to boot. I will re-phrase that – he was also devoted to his mother. So that was all right, then. The twins were born in the East End in 1933. Noted as particularly vicious street fighters from an early age, they both turned professional boxers at the age of seventeen, before being called up for National Service a year later. But the war had ended and the peacetime army was probably distressingly non-violent for their tastes. They deserted within six months, eventually being dishonourably discharged. They found their true vocation at an early age – Reggie got two years' probation for grievous bodily harm on a policeman in 1950 and Ronnie followed his brotherly example in 1953, getting a month in prison for assaulting a police officer. It was during his first spell in prison that Ronnie's mental illness was diagnosed – he was a chronic paranoid schizophrenic, though this apparently did not get in the way of his release at the end of his sentence.

In the years following their release, they built up a criminal empire in the East End, operated from the Regal snooker hall. While Ronnie was serving his first term of imprisonment, the business had been in serious danger of going legitimate. Reggie set up a dining club, the Double R, and he became accustomed to being the genial smoking-jacketed host. He could possibly have become a proper businessman. But Ronnie's increasingly violent tendencies needed a more active outlet and they went on to build up a substantial business, based on fraud and intimidation. Frauds alone were estimated to have netted them £100,000 in 1962. At one point Ronnie even tried to put the bite for protection money on a club they already owned.

They muscled in on Peter Rachman's Notting Hill rent collectors. Rachman at first did not take them seriously and made the mistake of trying to pay them with a rubber cheque. He was soon made to realise the error of his ways, and had to find a way of paying them off rather quickly. Thus it was that the Krays came to be the proprietors of Esmeralda's Barn, a plush Knightsbridge casino for which they paid Rachman a remarkably low rent. Although this initially earned a substantial (for the time) £80,000 a year, the Krays interfered so incompetently with the running of the business – exceeding credit limits and attracting clientele who were, to say the least, 'not quite from the top drawer' – that it eventually went bust.

All the time the police were trying to make more serious charges against them stick. But it seemed as if the Krays, who modelled themselves on the Chicago gangsters of the 1930s, led a charmed existence. In April 1965 the twins and another man, Edward Smith, went on trial accused of obtaining protection money with menaces from the Hideaway Club in Soho's Gerrard Street. They were acquitted on the instructions of the judge, after one of the key prosecution witnesses proved to be unreliable.

'I sewed mail bags with Reggie Kray' became an invaluable ice-breaker at the best parties

Reggie celebrated his escape by getting married two weeks later. For someone who allegedly doted on his mother (whom the twins referred to as 'Our Queen'), he proved to be hardly the most caring of husbands. He set the scene for their married life on his wedding night by locking his new bride in their Athens hotel bedroom, while he went out to get drunk. She took an overdose and killed herself two years later.

Despite (or perhaps because of) their fearsome reputation, an air of glamour seemed to surround the Krays. Show business personalities and aristocracy went out of their way to socialise with them and even the most casual acquaintances seemed to feel they earned some kudos through their slight association – 'I sewed mail bags with Reggie Kray' became an invaluable ice-breaker at the best parties. A man named George Dixon, who had upset Ronnie, had the terrifying experience of having Ronnie point a gun at his head *and pull the trigger*. The gun jammed. Ronnie took the bullet out and handed it to his quivering would-be victim, saying 'This has got your name on it.' Whatever it was Dixon did, he never did it again. He subsequently wore the bullet on a chain around his neck and no doubt dined out on the experience for years afterwards.

Within three months of the Hideaway Club trial, it was Charles's turn in front of the Beak. He and one Cornelius Whitehead were charged with the murder of Frank Mitchell (also known as 'the Mad Axeman' – though only to his closest friends). Mitchell was a former member of the Firm who had spent eighteen of his first thirty-two years in detention of one kind or another. It would be fair to say that the Krays did not hire him for his brains. He was at this time spending an indefinite spell at Dartmoor where he was apparently known as a 'trusty' (though how anyone with the nickname 'Mad Axeman' can earn trusty status beggars belief). Amazingly, the authorities let him go out for unsupervised nature rambles on the moor, visiting the shops and the local pub, so springing him from prison was hardly the organisational challenge of a lifetime.

The story goes that Mitchell grew increasingly fretful while in hiding and the Krays were getting worried about the growing risks involved. On Christmas Eve 1966 a van turned up to collect Mitchell from his hiding place. According to one of the gang who later turned Queen's evidence, two gunmen were waiting for Mitchell inside the van and shot him several times. The Krays' version is that Mitchell is now living safely abroad somewhere. Whatever the truth, Mitchell was never seen alive again – but his body was never found. Once again, the accused were found not guilty. Ronnie and Reggie were later charged, with another man, both for Mitchell's murder and for helping him to escape from prison. But before they could face these charges, they were brought to court in March 1969 for the murders of Jack (the Hat) McVitie and George Cornell, conspiracy to murder and assorted minor crimes (such as Ronnie's attempt at cosmetic surgery – with a red-hot poker – on the face of a man who had upset him).

The Cornell murder stemmed from a period of gang warfare between the Krays and another leading bunch of East End mobsters, the Richardson Gang. This culminated in an Al Capone-style shoot-out in March 1966, at a club called Mr Smith and the Witch Doctor. At the end of it, the power of the Richardson Gang was broken. Key gang members had been dispatched to the morgue, the hospital or into the arms of the police. Cornell was one of the last remaining Richardson Gang members still in business, and Ronnie went straight round to see him, demanding a slice of his pornography business. Cornell rejected his proposition, calling Ronnie Kray 'a fat poofter' into the bargain. He was factually correct in both respects – Ronnie was a self-confessed homosexual – but whoever coined the phrase 'honesty is the best policy' probably did not have in mind casting aspersions on Ronnie Kray's waistline or sexual predilections.

Shortly after this, on 8 March 1966, Cornell was having a drink at the Blind Beggar pub on the Mile End Road. It was a venue well known to the criminal underworld – seventy years before, it had been the headquarters of a criminal gang which took its name from the pub. Ronnie Kray walked in and Cornell just had time to say 'Well, look who's here!' before Ronnie shot him between the eyes in front of several dozen witnesses. The pub emptied with remarkable rapidity, the would-be witnesses suddenly remembering urgent prior engagements and finding that the alcohol had caused their recollection of the dramatic events of the evening to become remarkably vague.

The alcohol had caused their recollection of the dramatic events of the evening to become remarkably vague

Jack (the Hat – worn to cover his premature baldness) McVitie was a drunk and a drug user, whom Ronnie rather unwisely hired to kill somebody, giving him a gun and £100 for his trouble. McVitie bungled the operation and moreover was unable to repay the money. Ronnie's mental illness was by this time running out of control and he had been taunting his twin brother to match his execution of Cornell: 'I done my one. When are you going to do yours? Are you too soft?'

McVitie sealed his own fate by getting blind drunk and turning up at the Krays' Regency Club with a sawn-off shotgun, threatening to blast the twins. Even more unwisely, he accepted an invitation to a party with the Krays, who offered him 'all the booze and birds he could handle', at an address in Stoke Newington. As McVitie entered, ready to party, Ronnie grabbed him and Reggie tried to shoot him. But the gun jammed and McVitie tried to make his escape by jumping through a window, which happened to be closed at the time. The Krays pulled him back and, with Ronnie taunting him, Reggie stabbed McVitie in the face, the stomach and the chest, finally skewering him to the floor through his throat. McVitie's body was never found, though he is now thought to be in the care of the Department of Transport, forming part of a motorway flyover.

The Firm was starting to show signs of falling apart. Ronnie's erratic behaviour created fear and suspicion and led to a number of associates talking to the police. In a raid on 8 May 1968 the police arrested the gang, with sixty-eight detectives hitting twenty-four separate houses. The trial which followed was one of the longest and most expensive in criminal history. But at last the police got a result, with Ronnie being found guilty of both murders and Reggie of McVitie's. The judge sentenced them to life, recommending that they serve at least thirty years – the longest sentence ever handed out for murder. For good measure brother Charles got ten years as an accessory to the murder, making it a bad day all round for the family. Ronnie and Reggie were later acquitted of the Mitchell murder, though this was by now somewhat academic to any travel plans they might have had.

Despite his homosexuality Ronnie was to marry in 1985. Elaine Mildiner, at twenty-eight years old many years his junior, was at first not at all put off by the fact that her new husband was both gay and residing in Broadmoor at the time. This did, however, put something of a dampener on any honeymoon arrangements she might have planned. It will come as no surprise to learn that the marriage was never consummated. Five months after the wedding, she stopped visiting him and in 1989 Ronnie got a divorce on the grounds of her desertion. But such was the magic of Ronnie and the Kray name that he married again shortly afterwards. His new wife wrote a necessarily rather brief book about their married life together, in which she spoke touchingly of Ronnie's love of poetry and painting. She also talked about his mental problems. For most of the time he was apparently the perfect gentleman described earlier, but from time to time he felt the interludes of paranoia coming on. At such times he apparently liked to have his medication increased and to be left alone – something which I suspect few even in Broadmoor dared deny him.

Elaine Mildiner, at twenty-eight years old many years his junior, was at first not at all put off by the fact that her new husband was both gay and residing in Broadmoor

EMIL SAVUNDRA

The Fire Auto and Marine Insurance Company seemed to insurance experts to be too good to be true. The rates it was able to charge defied the laws of the actuary. The reason for this was that it *was* too good to be true. When it collapsed in 1966, it had debts of £2.5 millions and some 45,000 unpaid claims outstanding. Around 400,000 people were left uninsured. The company's managing director was a 43-year-old Ceylonese-born businessman, Dr Emil Savundra. He had arrived in England in 1950 with nothing to declare, as Oscar Wilde had previously put it, but his genius. In short, he had an arrogance that was truly breathtaking. He also brought with him an established track record as a swindler, having conducted large-scale frauds in Costa Rica, Goa, China and Ghana. Even his title 'Doctor' was self-awarded. However, it took him until 1954 to be arrested for fraud by the British authorities. He was deported to Belgium in 1956 and given five years' imprisonment there, until a Catholic cardinal interceded for his release on the grounds of ill-health (Savundra found that his other activities were no impediment to his being a staunch Catholic).

Fire Auto and Marine was set up in 1963, with Savundra becoming a director shortly afterwards. It was not conceived as a fraudulent venture, or so the defence counsel claimed at the trial. It used what was considered at the time to be one of the world's most advanced computer systems of its type. It could generate a policy in six seconds and did away with the need for cover notes. It was this that Savundra claimed enabled him to undercut all the competition and in his estimation it was set to transform the insurance market. He modestly regarded himself as one of the world's greatest geniuses.

There were signs that all was not well with the company as early as March 1965. Savundra issued instructions to his staff to limit payments on claims to £10,000 a week, and the backlog of unsettled claims started to build up. But this did not put a dampener on Savundra's own lifestyle. That year he spent £13,000 through his expense account at Harrods alone; he was running five Rolls-Royces and living in sumptuous luxury. Savundra's vehicle for salting away the money of the policy-holders was a Liechtenstein-based merchant bank called Merchants and Finance Trust. Without telling the board of the insurance company, Savundra and a fellow director paid large sums of Fire Auto and Marine's money to MFT, which the bank then lent to them personally on remarkably generous terms. This was not unconnected with the fact that Savundra himself had created the bank – attempts by investigators to locate its registered office in Liechtenstein ran into some difficulty.

Savundra described himself as 'God's own lounge lizard turned swindler'. He pursued sexual gratification as avidly as he did easy money. A criminal named James Pyper had supplied him with a love-nest near Marble Arch and a list of call girls. He met Stephen Ward, of Profumo scandal fame, and knowing of his reputation for arranging what we will call 'romantic liaisons' Savundra told Ward of his partiality for blondes and redheads 'with very long legs and very white skin'. Ward introduced him to Mandy Rice-Davies, to their mutual satisfaction.

Savundra described himself as 'God's own lounge lizard turned swindler'

In June 1966 a book called *The Gnomes of Zurich* was published, containing what Savundra described as a 'highly libellous' chapter about his business activities. Purely by coincidence, Savundra's health took a turn for the worse just at this time. Indeed, the very day after the book's publication, Savundra felt obliged to resign from the company 'for health reasons'. Within a fortnight, Fire Auto and Marine was being wound up. After the collapse of the business, irate customers waited for the law to take its course against the man who had swindled them, but nothing happened. No fewer than three newspapers investigated his business dealings, but no action was forthcoming from the Board of Trade. It appeared that the part of the law relating to Savundra's particular fraud was weak and they were not confident of obtaining a conviction. Significantly, none of the newspapers had managed to get Savundra to answer the charges that had been laid against him.

The breakthrough came early in February 1967, when the David Frost television programme ran a sketch that was a thinly veiled attack on the Fire Auto and Marine saga. After the programme the producers were surprised to receive a telephone call from Savundra himself, saying how much he had enjoyed the item. They in turn asked Savundra whether he himself would like to appear on the show and, to their amazement, he accepted. More amazing still, he failed to have second thoughts on the matter in the week that followed and turned up at the studio displaying what Frost described as 'towering self-confidence'. The subsequent interview gave birth to the phrase 'trial by television'. Bernard Levin describes the event thus:

> Savundra cut a figure so unpleasant that the normal sympathy of any audience for the victim of television bullying was instantly alienated, particularly since Frost had taken care to pack the audience with a number of Savundra's victims, including widows whose husbands had been killed while insured with Savundra's firm and who had found that there was no insurance forthcoming.

I am not going to cross swords with the peasants

Savundra disclaimed any moral responsibility for what had happened on the grounds that he had managed to sell out his share in the business before the crash, and he tried to use the interview to plug his forthcoming memoirs. At one point, he was asked 'It's all fun to you, isn't it?' to which he readily agreed. When some of the cheated widows challenged him, he tried to use the deaths of their husbands as some kind of debating point and when cornered by them over some of his activities, said: 'I am not going to cross swords with the peasants.' By the end of the interview, the weakness of his case had been brutally exposed and the cheering audience were yelling 'Good old Frosty!' Frost himself was so furious at Savundra's behaviour that he stormed off the stage before the closing credits had finished, rather than having to stay and exchange pleasantries with the man. That evening the Director of Public Prosecutions phoned the Fraud Squad and told them that they must find something to charge Savundra with if the law was not to be made to look an ass. With a week, Savundra was arrested. He was charged on two counts of fraud and was reduced to signing on at the Finchley employment exchange. Before the case opened, checks were made to ensure that there were no Fire Auto and Marine policyholders among the jury.

At the trial it was estimated that Savundra and his fellow defendant had helped themselves to something like £600,000 of the company's money. Although civil proceedings were started to try to recover some of it, no evidence was found of large sums having been salted away. It had all gone on extravagant living. The trial itself turned out to be a media circus. Savundra collapsed in the dock on a couple of occasions, but at other times was his usual arrogant self – to the extent that the judge had to intervene at one point to protect a defence counsel from Savundra's harangues. There was talk about Fire Auto and Marine's money being used to buy a nudist colony at Hastings and claims that Savundra's co-defendant was using a former German E-boat for smuggling.

In March 1968 Emil Savundra was sentenced to eight years in prison and a fine of £50,000. Fellow director Stuart de Quincy Walker got five years and a fine of £30,000. At his appeal Savundra's lawyer raised the claim of trial by television. The appeal judge Lord Justice Salmon dismissed the appeal, but took the opportunity to attack the Frost programme, saying that they must have known that a prosecution was imminent, and that contempt of court was not limited to cases where charges had actually been laid. Dark threats were made about prosecuting the broadcasters, should there be any repetition of the offence. This seems rather an unreasonable stance. It is easy enough to find out whether charges have been laid, but how does one establish that they are 'imminent'? What counts as imminent? Certainly, none of the journalists who had been following the case with increasing frustration for the past year thought they were about to see a prosecution. Even the Board of Trade, when questioned privately about the plan to run the broadcast, raised no objection to it. It could well be argued that, without the stimulus of the television programme, Savundra might have got away with his crimes.

One consequence of the Savundra case was that the law relating to insurance companies was tightened. The minimum sum required to start up a company was raised from £50,000 to £250,000 and the Board of Trade was given greater powers of control and investigation. Customers should from then have been safe from a collapse as spectacular as that of Fire Auto and Marine. Savundra was released from prison in 1974, and died two years later.

RONNIE BIGGS AND THE GREAT TRAIN ROBBERS

At ten to seven on the evening of 7 August 1963 a travelling post office left Glasgow station for London. The second of its coaches was stuffed full with 128 bags of English banknotes being transferred back to England. By the early hours of the following day, it was passing through an area known as Sears Cross in Buckinghamshire, when a red signal caused it to stop. Driver Jack Mills, aged fifty-eight, sent his assistant out to see what was going on – but the man who got back into the cab a few moments later was not his colleague.

There was talk about Fire Auto and Marine's money being used to buy a nudist colony at Hastings and claims that Savundra's co-defendant was using a former German E-boat for smuggling

Police search the scene of the Great Train Robbery for clues.

Mills fought bravely with the intruder until he was knocked down by a blow to the head with an iron bar. Other members of the gang then started breaking into the high value coach. The GPO employees inside thought about resistance, until one of the gang shouted something that sounded like 'get the guns'. The GPO staff thereafter wisely decided to lie down in the corner and avert their gaze as the robbers removed the bags. The robber who guarded them made friendly conversation, asked their names and allowed them to smoke. He even said that he would take their addresses and send them a few pounds when it was all over. He did not go so far as divulging his own identity, but those involved would soon become familiar enough with the name of Ronald Biggs, whose subsequent history made him the best known of the robbers.

When the gang got back to their hideaway at Leatherslade Farm, it took them an entire day to share out the proceeds. In those days the largest note in circulation was worth £5 and their total haul amounted to £2,631,784. Biggs himself came away with between £120,000 and £158,000, depending on whether you believe him or his former wife.

For some reason the Great British Public took these criminals to their hearts and regarded them as some kind of heroes. One reason for this might have been that it was seen – wrongly – as a victimless crime. It was money taken from excessively rich banks, one of which – it turned out, to additional public glee – had not even bothered to insure their share of the shipment. Victimless it was not. Jack Mills, the train driver, was permanently disabled by the blow he received, and died in the first weeks of the 1970s. A collection for him was only belatedly started in 1969, and did not even raise as much as two of the gang members' wives had got for selling their stories to the newspapers.

A second reason was that the public were in an anarchic mood, welcoming anything that appeared to be anti-authority, for their faith in the Establishment had been sorely tested of late. We had just failed –

"You are, perhaps, one of the Great Train Robbers!"

Don't be a check point charlie.

You can sit back while Lloyds take care of some holiday problems for you. For example, money.

Travellers cheques mean that you keep a check on your money abroad. If your pockets aren't permanently bulging with cash, you won't be tempted to spend money on all those beautiful foreign bargains you don't really need . . . you may even end up with some spare money at the end of your holiday. What's more, you can use travellers cheques travelling around the U.K.—you can cash them in the branches of other banks as well as Lloyds.

You are sure to need some ready money for your immediate needs on landing. Foreign currency can be obtained through any branch and at larger branches on demand.

In addition, Lloyds will help you with all the formalities of getting a passport—all you have to do is visit your local Lloyds Bank manager and give him the relevant details. Just another way in which Lloyds help you to save time and energy.

Times are hard with the £50 limit, but your Lloyds manager can help you with useful information on the latest regulations—for example, if you're taking a car abroad, you're allowed an extra £25.

When you go to Lloyds, be sure to pick up their 'Going Abroad' booklet—a fund of useful information. Call in at your local Lloyds branch now.

Lloyds Bank looks after people like you

The Great Train Robbers even caught the imagination of the advertisers, and the cinema.

courtesy of General de Gaulle – to get into the Common Market; the sordid web of deceit and ineptitude that was the Philby spy saga had just come out and the public entertainment of the Profumo affair was just about coming to an end. The public loved the Great Train Robbery, as it came to be called, especially when overseas papers were forced to acknowledge that Britain could still lead the world in something.

Seventeen people were said to have taken part in the robbery though three of them were never even named, let alone caught. But despite the assistance of deeply unhelpful press speculation as to their identity – it was variously said to have been masterminded by a miser from Brighton, a dubious baronet and the IRA – the police were soon on their trail. Their hideaway at the farm was found and members of the gang started abandoning large sums of money that had become too hot to handle. This merely added a treasure hunt to the carnival atmosphere surrounding the case.

Biggs' capture was – for him – particularly unfortunate. His brother had died on the night he left home and his wife had unwittingly sent the Wiltshire Constabulary to the woodcutting site where he had told her – not entirely accurately – that he was working, to inform him of his bereavement. They could not find him there, nor on any other woodcutting site in the county. Biggs was not only bereaved, his alibi was blown – and then his fingerprints turned up on the tomato sauce bottle at Leatherslade Farm. Ronnie's fingerprints were well known to the authorities.

Within two weeks Biggs had been arrested and in April 1964 twelve members of the gang were found guilty of taking part in the robbery. They were given heavy gaol sentences. Biggs was given thirty years, the same as the Kray twins. But like so many other people in this book who ended up in prison, Biggs did not find it too difficult to get out again. On 8 July 1965 a hired gang used the well-tried removals van and rope ladder technique to secure the release of Biggs and a number of other long-sentence prisoners from Wandsworth.

Biggs hid out in Bognor Regis, while some plastic surgery was carried out, and then he and his family made their way to Australia. But such was the enduring press interest in the robbery that Biggs' new identity was exposed by 1969. He was forced to flee again, this time to Brazil, the escape funded by the sale of his story to an Australian newspaper. The complex and often hilarious tale of the government's attempts to extradite Biggs from Brazil belongs – unhappily for our present purposes – to another decade. But at the time of writing this, Ronnie Biggs is still safely out of the reach of British justice.

A hired gang used the well-tried removals van and rope ladder technique to secure the release of Biggs and a number of other long-sentence prisoners from Wandsworth

A NOTE ON SOURCES

Every writer of history owes a debt to those who have covered the ground before them. I can do no more here than commend to you some of the most valuable sources of material for this book. My thanks go to them, and to others, too numerous to mention.

A lot of my material came from newspaper reports of the day, in both national and local papers from around the country. *Record Collector* magazine provided much useful information about a number of the pop stars of the period featured in the pop music chapter.

Benson, John, *The rise of the consumer society in Britain, 1880–1980* (Longman, 1994)

Bower, Tom, *The perfect English spy* (Heinemann, 1995)

Buchanan, Gary C. *Queen Elizabeth 2 – Past and Present* (1995)

Childs, David, *Britain since 1945: a political history* (Routledge, 1992)

——, *Britain since 1939 – progress & decline* (Macmillan, 1995)

Deacon, Richard, *Spyclopedia* (Macdonald, 1988)

Donovan, Paul, *The radio companion* (Grafton, 1992)

Edelstein, Andrew J. *The pop 1960s* (World Almanac Publications, 1985)

Frost, David, *Autobiography* (HarperCollins, 1993)

Gourvish, Terry & O'Day, Alan (eds), *Britain since 1945* (Macmillan, 1991)

Greaves, Jimmy, *The 1960s revisited* (Queen Anne Press, 1992)

Hardy, R.H.N., *Beeching – Champion of the railway?* (Ian Allan, 1989)

Hewison, Robert, *Too much – Art & society in the 60s* (Methuen, 1986)

Ivanov, Yevgeny, *The naked spy – Blake* (1992)

Knighton, Philip & Kennedy, Caroline, *An affair of state* (Cape, 1987)

Kray, Kate, *Married to the Krays* (Atlantic, 1992)

Larkin, Colin (ed.), *Guinness who's who of 1960s music* (Guinness, 1992)

Levin, Bernard, *The pendulum years* (Cape, 1970)

Lloyd, T.O. *Empire, welfare state, Europe – English history, 1906–1992* (OUP, 1993)

Macdonald, Ian, *Revolution in the head* (Fourth Estate, 1994)

Maitland, Sara (ed.), *Very Heaven* (Virago, 1988)

Morrison, Ann & Ian, *The A–Z of the 1960s* (Breedon Books, 1989)

Nawrat, Chris & Hutchings, Steve, *Sunday Times illustrated history of football* (Hamlyn, 1996)

Nuttgens, Patrick, *The home front* (BBC, 1989)

Obelkevich, James & Catterall, Peter, *Understanding post-war British society* (Routledge, 1994)

Parris, Matthew, *Great parliamentary scandals* (Robson, 1995)

Paterson, Peter, *Tired and emotional* (Chatto & Windus, 1993)

Richardson, Jeffrey & Ball, Desmond, *The ties that bind* (Unwin Hyman, 1985)

Rositzke, Harry, *KGB, the eyes of Russia* (Sidgwick & Jackson, 1982)

Saggar, Shamit, *Race and politics in Britain* (Harvester/Wheatsheaf, 1992)

Small, Steve, *The Guinness complete Grand Prix who's who* (Guinness, 1994)

Spittles, Brian, *Britain since 1960 – an introduction* (Macmillan, 1995)

Summers, Anthony & Dorril, Stephen, *Honeytrap – the secret worlds of Stephen Ward* (Weidenfeld & Nicolson, 1987)

Szatmary, David, *A time to rock* (Schirmer, 1996)

Turnill, Reginald, *Celebrating Concorde* (Ian Allan, 1994)

Vahimagi, Tise (ed.), *British Television* (OUP/BFI, 1996)

Walker, Martin, *The cold war* (Fourth Estate, 1993)

Whitehouse, Mary, *Quite contrary* (Sidgwick & Jackson, 1993)

INDEX